MacArthur
BIBLE STUDIES

HEBREWS

Christ—Perfect Sacrifice, Perfect Priest

JOHN
MacARTHUR

Hebrews

Table of Contents

THE EPISTLE TO THE HEBREWS

Introduction

When the various New Testament books were formally brought together into one collection shortly after A.D. 100, the titles were added for convenience. This epistle bears the traditional Greek title "To the Hebrews," which was attested to by at least the second century A.D. Within the epistle itself, however, there is no identification of the recipients as either Hebrews (Jews) or Gentiles. Since the epistle is filled with references to Hebrew history and religion and does not address any particular Gentile or pagan practice, the traditional title has been maintained.

Author and Date

The author of Hebrews is unknown. Paul, Barnabas, Silas, Apollos, Luke, Philip, Priscilla, Aquila, and Clement of Rome have been suggested by different scholars, but the epistle's vocabulary, style, and various literary characteristics do not clearly support any particular claim. It is significant that the writer includes himself among those people who had received confirmation of Christ's message from others (2:3). That would seem to rule out someone like Paul who claimed that he had received such confirmation directly from God and not from men (Gal. 1:12). Whoever the author was, he preferred citing Old Testament references from the Greek Old Testament (LXX) rather than from the Hebrew text. Even the early church expressed various opinions on authorship, and current scholarship admits the puzzle still has no solution. Therefore, it seems best to accept the epistle's anonymity. Ultimately, of course, the author was the Holy Spirit (2 Pet. 1:21).

The use of the present tense in 5:1–4; 7:21, 23, 27–28; 8:3–5, 13; 9:6–9, 13, 25; 10:1, 3–4, 8, 11; and 13:10–11 would suggest that the Levitical priesthood and sacrificial system were still in operation when the epistle was composed. Since the temple was destroyed by General (later Emperor) Titus Vespasian in A.D. 70, the epistle must have been written prior to that date. In addition, it may be noted that Timothy had just been released from prison (13:23) and that persecution was becoming severe (10:32–39; 12:4; 13:3). These details suggest a date for the epistle of around A.D. 67–69.

Background and Setting

Emphases on the Levitical priesthood and on sacrifices, as well as the absence of any reference to the Gentiles, support the conclusion that a community of Hebrews was the recipient of the epistle. Although these Hebrews were primarily converts to Christ, there were probably a number of unbelievers in their midst who were attracted by the message of salvation but had not yet made a full commitment of faith in Christ (see Interpretive Challenges). One thing is clear from the contents of the epistle: The community of Hebrews was facing the possibility of intensified persecution (10:32–39; 12:4). As they confronted this possibility, the Hebrews were tempted to cast aside any identification with Christ. They may have considered demoting Christ from God's Son to a mere angel. Such a precedent had already been set by the Qumran community of messianic Jews living near the Dead Sea. They had dropped out of society, established a religious commune, and included the worship of angels in their brand of reformed Judaism. The Qumran community had even gone so far as to claim that the angel Michael was higher in status than the coming Messiah. These kinds of doctrinal aberrations could explain the emphasis in Hebrews chapter one on the superiority of Christ over the angels.

Possible locations for the recipients of the epistle include Palestine, Egypt, Italy, Asia Minor, and Greece. The community that was the primary recipient may have circulated the epistle among those of Hebrew background in neighboring areas and churches. Those believers probably had not seen Christ personally. Apparently, they had been evangelized by "those who heard" Christ and whose ministries had been authenticated "with signs and wonders, with various miracles" (2:3–4). Thus the recipients could have been in a church outside Judea and Galilee or in a church in those areas, but established among people in the generation following those who had been eyewitnesses of Christ. The congregation was not new or untaught ("by this time you ought to be teachers") yet some of them still needed "milk and not solid food" (5:12).

"Those from Italy" (13:24) is an ambiguous reference since it could mean either those who had left Italy and were living elsewhere, or those who were still in Italy and being singled out as native residents of that country. Greece or Asia Minor must also be considered because of the apparently early establishment of the church there, and because of the consistent use of the LXX.

The generation of Hebrews receiving this epistle had practiced the Levitical sacrifices at the temple in Jerusalem. Jews living in exile had substituted the synagogue for the temple but still felt a deep attraction to the temple worship. Some had the means to make regular pilgrimages to the temple in Jerusalem. The writer of this epistle emphasized the superiority of Christianity over Judaism and the superiority of Christ's once-for-all sacrifice over the repeated and imperfect Levitical sacrifices observed in the temple.

Historical and Theological Themes

Since the book of Hebrews is grounded in the work of the Levitical priesthood, an understanding of the book of Leviticus is essential for properly interpreting Hebrews. Israel's sin had continually interrupted God's fellowship with His chosen and covenant people, Israel. Therefore, He graciously and sovereignly established a system of sacrifices that symbolically represented the inner repentance of sinners and His divine forgiveness. However, the need for sacrifices never ended because the people and priests continued to sin. The need of all humankind was for a perfect priest and a perfect sacrifice that would once and for all actually remove sin. God's provision for that perfect priest and sacrifice in Christ is the central message of Hebrews.

The epistle to the Hebrews is a study in contrast, between the imperfect and incomplete provisions of the Old Covenant, given under Moses, and the infinitely better provisions of the New Covenant offered by the perfect high priest, God's only Son and the Messiah, Jesus Christ. Included in the "better" provisions are a better hope, testament, promise, sacrifice, substance, country, and resurrection. Those who belong to the New Covenant dwell in a completely new and heavenly atmosphere, they worship a heavenly Savior, have a heavenly calling, receive a heavenly gift, are citizens of a heavenly country, look forward to a heavenly Jerusalem, and have their very names written in heaven.

One of the key theological themes in Hebrews is that all believers now have direct access to God under the New Covenant and, therefore, may approach the throne of God boldly (4:16; 10:22). One's hope is in the very presence of God, into which he follows the Savior (6:19–20; 10:19–20). The primary teaching symbolized by the tabernacle service was that believers under the covenant of law did not have direct access to the presence of God (9:8) but were shut out of the Most Holy Place. The Book of Hebrews may briefly be summarized in this way: Believers in Jesus Christ, God's perfect sacrifice for sin, have the perfect high priest through whose ministry everything is new and better than under the covenant of law.

This epistle is more than a doctrinal treatise, however. It is intensely practical in its application to everyday living (see chap. 13). The writer himself even refers to his letter as a "word of exhortation" (13:22; see Acts 13:15). Exhortations designed to stir the readers into action are found throughout the text. Those exhortations are given in the form of six warnings:

1. Warning against drifting from "the things we have heard" (2:1–4)
2. Warning against disbelieving the "voice" of God (3:7–14)
3. Warning against degenerating from "the elementary principles of Christ" (5:11—6:20)
4. Warning against despising "the knowledge of the truth" (10:26–39)
5. Warning against devaluing "the grace of God" (12:15–17)
6. Warning against departing from Him "who speaks" (12:25–29)

Another significant aspect of this epistle is its clear exposition of selected Old Testament passages. The writer was clearly a skilled expositor of the Word of God. His example is instructive for preachers and teachers:

1:1 and 2:4	Exposition of verses from Psalms; 2 Samuel 7; Deuteronomy 32
2:5 and 18	Exposition of Psalm 8:4, 6
3:1 and 4:13	Exposition of Psalm 95:7, 11
4:14 and 7:28	Exposition of Psalm 110:4
8:1 and 10:18	Exposition of Jeremiah 31:31, 34
10:32 and 12:3	Exposition of Habakkuk 2:3–4
12:4 and 13	Exposition of Proverbs 3:11–12
12:18 and 29	Exposition of Exodus 19, 20

Interpretive Challenges

A proper interpretation of this epistle requires the recognition that it addresses three distinct groups of Jews: (1) believers; (2) unbelievers who were intellectually convinced of the gospel; and (3) unbelievers who were attracted by the gospel and the person of Christ but who had reached no final conviction about Him. Failure to acknowledge these groups leads to interpretations inconsistent with the rest of Scripture.

The primary group addressed were Hebrew Christians who suffered rejection and persecution by fellow Jews (10:32–34), although none as yet had been martyred (12:4). The letter was written to give them encouragement and confidence in Christ, their Messiah and high priest. They were an immature group of believers who were tempted to hold on to the symbolic and spiritually powerless rituals and traditions of Judaism.

The second group addressed were Jewish unbelievers who were convinced of the basic truths of the gospel but who had not placed their faith in Jesus Christ as their own Savior and Lord. They were intellectually persuaded but spiritually uncommitted. These unbelievers are addressed in such passages as 2:1–3; 6:4–6; 10:26–29; and 12:15–17.

The third group addressed were Jewish unbelievers who were not convinced of the gospel's truth but had had some exposure to it. Chapter 9 is largely devoted to them (see especially vv. 11, 14–15, 27–28).

By far the most serious interpretive challenge is found in 6:4–6. The phrase "once enlightened" is often taken to refer to Christians, and the accompanying warning taken to indicate the danger of losing their salvation if "they fall away" and "crucify again for themselves the Son of God." But there is no mention of their being saved and they are not described with any terms that apply only to believers (such as holy, born again, righteous, or saints). This problem arises from inaccurately identifying the spiritual condition of the ones being addressed. In this case, they were unbelievers who had been exposed to God's redemptive truth and perhaps had made a profession of faith, but they had not exercised genuine saving faith. In 10:26, the reference once again is to nominal Christians who apostatize, not to genuine believers who are often incorrectly thought to lose their salvation because of their sins.

OUTLINE

I. The Superiority of Jesus Christ's Position (1:1–4:13)
    A. A Better Name (1:1–3)
    B. Better than the Angels (1:4–2:18)
        1. A greater messenger (1:4–14)
        2. A greater message (2:1–18)
            a. A greater salvation (2:1–4)
            b. A greater savior (2:5–18)
    C. Better than Moses (3:1–19)
    D. A Better Rest (4:1–13)
II. The Superiority of Jesus Christ's Priesthood (4:14–7:28)
    A. Christ as High Priest (4:14–5:10)
    B. Exhortation to Full Commitment to Christ (5:11–6:20)
    C. Christ's Priesthood like Melchizedek's (7:1–28)
III. The Superiority of Jesus Christ's Priestly Ministry (8:1–10:18)
    A. Through a Better Covenant (8:1–13)
    B. In a Better Sanctuary (9:1–12)
    C. By a Better Sacrifice (9:13–10:18)
IV. The Superiority of the Believer's Privileges (10:19–12:29)
    A. Saving Faith (10:19–25)
    B. False Faith (10:26–39)
    C. Genuine Faith (11:1–3)
    D. Heroes of the Faith (11:4–40)
    E. Persevering Faith (12:1–29)
V. The Superiority of Christian Behavior (13:1–21)
    A. In Relation to Others (13:1–3)
    B. In Relation to Ourselves (13:4–9)
    C. In Relation to God (13:10–21)
VI. Postscript (13:22–25)

Christ: Better than the Angels

Opening Thought

1) If you went to a busy metropolitan area at lunch-time and conducted "man on the street" interviews with passersby, asking the question, "Who is Jesus Christ?" what sort of responses do you think you would get?

_____

_____

_____

2) Why do you think most people are willing to talk publicly about religious figures like Buddha, Mohammed, and Confucius, and yet get agitated and upset when the name of Jesus Christ is injected into the conversation?

_____

_____

_____

3) What do you think is behind the tremendous resurgence of societal interest in angels over the last few years?

_____

_____

4) What do you think of those who fill their evangelistic appeals with warnings of dire consequences for rejecting Christ?

_____

_____

Background of the Passage

As stated in the Introduction, the over-arching theme of Hebrews is the supremacy or preeminence of Christ. He is better than all that was before. He is better than any Old Testament character. He is superior to any Old Testament institution. He is greater than any Old Testament ritual. He is better than any Old Testament sacrifice. He is better than anyone and everything else.

The writer immediately gets to his main point. In the first three verses of the epistle, he sums up all that he intends to say: Christ is the pure revelation of God, the epitome of all truth, and more. God has fully and completely expressed Himself in Christ. These verses either mention or allude to a number of the unique attributes of Christ—His heirship, His creatorship, His glory, His very essence, His governance of the universe, His sacrifice, His exaltation.

The remainder of the first two chapters are focused on arguing that Christ is superior to angels. Because of the Talmudic writings and popular rabbinical teachings, the Jewish people at the time this epistle was written had begun to embellish the basic Old Testament teachings about angels. The result was that a number of dangerous misconceptions had begun to spread, and in the Jewish mind, angels had become extremely exalted, immeasurably important, very nearly worshiped. If the writer of Hebrews was going to persuade his fellow Jews that Christ is the Mediator of a better covenant than the one given through Moses, he would have to demonstrate, among other things, that Christ is superior to the angels (1:4–14).

Such truth demands a response; this leads to the warning of 2:1–4—to the unconvinced Jews reading or hearing the epistle—not to neglect so great a salvation. There is only one real Savior who can salvage man's lost destiny (2:5–9); only one perfect Savior (2:9–18). He is Jesus Christ.

Bible Passage

Read 1:1–2:18, noting the key words and definitions to the right of the passage.

Hebrews 1:1–2:18

¹ *God, who at various times and in various ways spoke in time past to the fathers by the prophets,*

various times (v. 1)—The meaning is "many portions" (as of books). Over the course of possibly eighteen hundred years (from Job, about 2200 B.C., to

² *has in these last days spoken to us by His Son,*
whom He has appointed heir of all things,
through whom also He made the worlds;

³ *who being the brightness of His glory and the*
express image of His person, and upholding all
things by the word of His power, when He had by
Himself purged our sins, sat down at the right
hand of the Majesty on high ,

⁴ *having become so much better than the angels, as*
He has by inheritance obtained a more excellent
name than they.

⁵ *For to which of the angels did He ever say:*
"You are My Son,
Today I have begotten You"?
And again:
"I will be to Him a Father,
And He shall be to Me a Son"?

⁶ *But when He again brings the firstborn into the*
world, He says:
"Let all the angels of God worship Him."

⁷ *And of the angels He says:*
"Who makes His angels spirits
And His ministers a flame of fire."

⁸ *But to the Son He says:*
"Your throne, O God, is forever and ever;
A scepter of righteousness is the scepter of Your
Kingdom.

⁹ *You have loved righteousness and hated lawless-*
ness;
Therefore God, Your God, has anointed You
With the oil of gladness more than Your
companions."

¹⁰ *And:*
"You, LORD, in the beginning laid the foundation
of the earth,
And the heavens are the work of Your hands.

¹¹ *They will perish, but You remain;*
And they will all grow old like a garment;

¹² *Like a cloak You will fold them up,*

Nehemiah, about 400 B.C.) the Old Testament was written in thirty-nine different books reflecting different historical times, locations, cultures, and situations.

various ways (v. 1)—These included visions, symbols, and parables, written in both poetry and prose. Though the literary form and style varied, it was always God's revelation of what He wanted His people to know. The progressive revelation of the Old Testament described God's program of redemption and His will for His people (2 Tim. 3:16–17).

last days (v. 2)—Jews understood the "last days" to mean the time when Messiah (Christ) would come (see Jer. 33:14–16; Mic. 5:1, 2; Zech. 9:9, 16). The fulfillment of the messianic prophecies commenced with the advent of the Messiah. Since He came, it has been the "last days" (see James 5:8; 1 Pet. 1:20; 4:7; 1 John 2:18). In the past, God gave revelation through His prophets, but in these times, beginning with the Messiah's advent, God spoke the message of redemption through the Son.

heir (v. 2)—Everything that exists will ultimately come under the control of the Son of God, the Messiah. This "inheritance" is the full extension of the authority which the Father has given to the Son (see Dan. 7:13–14; Matt. 28:18) as the "firstborn" (see the note on v. 6).

worlds (v. 2)—The word can also be translated "ages." It refers to time, space, energy, and matter—the entire universe and everything that makes it function (see John 1:3).

brightness (v. 3)—The term is used only here in the New Testament. It expresses the

And they will be changed.
But You are the same,
And Your years will not fail."

¹³ *But to which of the angels has He ever said:*
"Sit at My right hand,
Till I make Your enemies Your footstool"?

¹⁴ *Are they not all ministering spirits sent forth to*
minister for those who will inherit salvation?

^{2:1} *Therefore we must give the more earnest heed to*
the things we have heard, lest we drift away.

² *For if the word spoken through angels proved*
steadfast, and every transgression and disobedi-
ence received a just reward,

³ *how shall we escape if we neglect so great a sal-*
vation, which at the first began to be spoken by
the Lord, and was confirmed to us by those who
heard Him,

⁴ *God also bearing witness both with signs and*
wonders, with various miracles, and gifts of the
Holy Spirit, according to His own will?

⁵ *For He has not put the world to come, of which*
we speak, in subjection to angels.

⁶ *But one testified in a certain place, saying:*
"What is man that You are mindful of him,
Or the son of man that You take care of him?

⁷ *You have made him a little lower than the angels;*
You have crowned him with glory and honor,
And set him over the works of Your hands.

⁸ *You have put all things in subjection under his*
feet."
For in that He put all in subjection under him,
He left nothing that is not put under him. But
now we do not yet see all things put under him.

⁹ *But we see Jesus, who was made a little lower*
than the angels, for the suffering of death
crowned with glory and honor, that He, by the
grace of God, might taste death for everyone.

¹⁰ *For it was fitting for Him, for whom are all*
things and by whom are all things, in bringing

concept of sending forth light or shining. The meaning "reflection" is not appropriate here. The Son is not just reflecting God's glory; He is God and radiates His own essential glory.

express image of His person (v. 3)—The term translated "express image" is used only here in the New Testament. In extrabiblical literature, it was employed for an engraving on wood, an etching in metal, a brand on animal hide, an impression in clay, and a stamped image on coins. "Person" is a word expressing nature, being, or essence. The Son is the perfect imprint, the exact representation of the nature and essence of God in time and space.

upholding (v. 3)—The universe and everything in it is constantly sustained by the Son's powerfully effective word (Col. 1:17). The term also conveys the concept of movement or progress—the Son of God directs all things toward the consummation of all things according to God's sovereign purpose. He who spoke all things into existence also sustains His creation and consummates His purpose by His word.

purged our sins (v. 3)—by His substitutionary sacrifice on the cross (see Rev. 1:5)

sat down at the right hand (v. 3)—The right hand is the place of power, authority, and honor (see v. 13). The seat that Christ has taken is the throne of God (8:1; 10:12; 12:2), where He rules as sovereign Lord. This depicts a victorious Savior, not a defeated martyr. While the primary thrust of this phrase is the enthronement of Christ, His sitting might also imply the completion of His atoning work.

having become (v. 4)—The Greek verb used here refers to a

many sons to glory, to make the captain of their salvation perfect through sufferings.

11 For both He who sanctifies and those who are being sanctified are all of one, for which reason He is not ashamed to call them brethren,

12 saying:

"I will declare Your name to My brethren;
In the midst of the assembly I will sing praise to You."

13 And again:

"I will put My trust in Him."
And again:
"Here am I and the children whom God has given Me."

14 Inasmuch then as the children have partaken of flesh and blood, He Himself likewise shared in the same, that through death He might destroy him who had the power of death, that is, the devil,

15 and release those who through fear of death were all their lifetime subject to bondage.

16 For indeed He does not give aid to angels, but He does give aid to the seed of Abraham.

17 Therefore, in all things He had to be made like His brethren, that He might be a merciful and faithful High priest in things pertaining to God, to make propitiation for the sins of the people.

18 For in that He Himself has suffered, being tempted, He is able to aid those who are tempted.

change of state, not a change of existence. The Son in His divine essence has eternally existed, but for a while He was made lower than the angels (2:9). Afterward He was exalted to high above the angels by virtue of what He had accomplished in His redemptive work.

angels (v. 4)—These are spirit beings created by God to minister to Him and do His bidding. The Jews held angels in very high regard as the high est beings next to God. The sect of Judaism which had established a community at Qumran taught that the archangel Michael's authority rivaled or surpassed that of the Messiah. The writer of Hebrews clearly disclaims any such concept. The Son of God is superior to the angels.

more excellent name (v. 4) —That name is Lord. No angel is Sovereign Lord (vv. 6, 13–14).

Son (v. 5)—This is a title of Christ expressing His essential deity and absolute equality with God. The begetting spoken of here refers to the relationship of the Son to the Father in eternity, not to a point in time. Christ had no beginning but is eternally of the same essence as the Father.

again (v. 6)—This adverb can be taken with "brings" as a reference to the second coming of Christ or with "says" to indicate yet another quotation from the Old Testament ("and again, when He brings the firstborn into the world, He says"; see v. 5; 2:13). The NKJV has chosen the former sense.

firstborn (v. 6)—This refers to prominence of position or title. Christ holds the highest position of sovereignty. As "firstborn" He is also set apart to the service of

God and, being preeminent, is entitled to the inheritance (see v. 2; Gen. 43:33; Ex. 13:2; 22:29; Deut. 21:17; Ps. 89:27).

Let all the angels (v. 6)—Since the angels are commanded to worship the Messiah, the Messiah must be superior to them. Five of the seven Old Testament passages quoted in this first chapter of Hebrews are in contexts related to the Davidic Covenant, which emphasizes the concepts of sonship, kingship, and kingdom. Although Deuteronomy 32:43 (quoted here from the Septuagint) is not in a Davidic Covenant context, it has an affinity to the teaching of Psalm 89:6 (a psalm of the Davidic Covenant), which declares that the heavenly beings themselves must recognize the lordship of God. Reference is made to "the first-born" in the introduction to the Deuteronomy quote. In addition, "firstborn" is mentioned in Psalm 89:27.

of the angels (v. 7)—The writer continues biblical proofs that the angels are subservient to the Son of God by citing Psalm 104:4. This is the only one of the seven Old Testament quotations in chapter 1 that has no connection at all to the Davidic Covenant. The quote merely defines the primary nature and purpose of angels.

He says (vv. 8–9)—Quoting from Psalm 45:6–7, the writer argues for the deity and the lordship of the Son over creation (see v. 3). The text is all the more significant since the declaration of the Son's deity is presented as the words of the Father Himself (see 1 John 5:20). It is clear that the writer of Hebrews had the three messianic offices in mind: Prophet (v. 1), Priest (v. 3), and King (v. 3, 8). Induction into those three offices required anointing (v. 9). The title Messiah (Christ) means "anointed one."

companions (v. 9)—The term is used only in Hebrews (3:1, 14; 6:4; 12:8) and in Luke 5:7. In this occurrence, it might refer to angels or to other men who were similarly anointed for their offices: the Old Testament prophets, priests, and kings. If the "oil of gladness" is the same as "oil of joy" referred to in Isaiah 61:3, the reference would clearly be to those who had mourned in Zion but who would one day be clothed with praise and called "trees of righteousness"—references to men, not angels. No matter how noble such men were, Christ is superior.

You, LORD (v. 10)—The Son who created the universe (John 1:1–3) will one day destroy the heavens and earth that He created, but He remains unchanged. Immutability is yet another characteristic of the divine essence. Once again the Old Testament testifies of the Son's deity.

"Sit at My right hand . . . " (vv. 13–14)—The writer reemphasizes the lordship of the Son by quoting Psalm 110:1. While Christ's destiny is to reign (see v. 3), the angels' destiny is to serve the recipients of salvation (see 1 Cor. 6:3). This is the seventh and final quotation from the Old Testament to bolster the argument that as Son and Lord the Messiah is superior to the angels.

enemies Your footstool (v. 13)—This quote from Psalm 110:1 is repeated at 10:13; Matthew 22:44; Mark 12:36; Luke 20:43; and Acts 2:35, and expresses the sovereignty of Christ over all (see Phil. 2:10).

earnest heed . . . drift away (v. 2:1)—Both phrases have nautical connotations. The first refers to mooring a ship, tying it up at the dock. The second was often used of a ship that had been allowed to drift past the harbor. The warning is to secure one's self to the truth of the gospel, being careful not to pass by the only harbor of salvation. The closest attention must be paid to these very serious matters of the Christian faith. The readers in their tendency to apathy are in danger of making shipwreck of their lives (see 6:19; see 1 Tim. 1:18).

if (v. 2)—The Greek term assumes a fulfilled condition and here carries the idea: "In view of the fact that. . . ."

angels (v. 2)—Angels were instrumental in bringing God's law to His people at Mount Sinai.

transgression and disobedience (v. 2)—The former means to step across the line, in an overt sin of commission. The latter carries the idea of shutting one's ears to God's commands, thereby committing a sin of omission. Both are willful, serious, and require just judgment.

how shall we escape (v. 3)—If disobedience to the older covenant of law brought swift judgment, how much more severe will be the judgment of disobedience to the New Covenant gospel of salvation, which was mediated by the Son who is superior to the angels (see Matt. 10:14–15; 11:20–24)? The messenger and message of the New Covenant are greater than the messengers and message of the older covenant. The greater the privilege, the greater the punishment for disobedience or neglect.

by those who heard Him (v. 3)—This phrase reveals the succession of evangelism. That generation of Hebrews would not have heard if the previous generation of witnesses had not passed the message along (see 1 Tim. 2:5–7).

signs . . . wonders . . . miracles . . . gifts (v. 4)—The supernatural powers demonstrated by Jesus and by His apostles were the Father's divine confirmation of the gospel of Jesus Christ, His Son (see John 10:38; Acts 2:22; Rom. 15:19; 1 Cor. 14:22). This authentication of the message was the purpose of such miraculous deeds.

the Holy Spirit (v. 4)—The epistle's first reference to the Holy Spirit refers in passing to His ministry of confirming the message of salvation by means of miraculous gifts. Mentioned elsewhere in the epistle are the Holy Spirit's involvement in the revelation of Scripture (3:7; 10:15), in teaching (9:8), in pre-salvation operations (6:4, perhaps His convicting work; 10:29, common grace), and in ministry to Christ (9:14).

world (v. 5)—The term refers to the inhabited earth. The reference is to the great millennial kingdom (see Zech. 14:9). Angels will not reign over the messianic kingdom.

in a certain place (v. 6)—This is not an indication that the writer was ignorant of the source of the quotation that follows. The location of the quotation is not as significant as its divine authorship. Perhaps it is significant that the author of Hebrews is not identified either. The writer may have desired that his readers understand that the Holy Spirit is the real author of all Scripture (see 2 Tim. 3:16).

man . . . son of man (v. 6)—Both refer to humankind, not to Christ. The passage asks why God would ever bother with man. As the following verses demonstrate (vv. 9, 10), the incarnation of Christ is the greatest proof of God's love and regard for humankind. Christ was not sent in the form of an angel. He was sent in the form of a man.

angels (v. 7)—Angels were given supernatural powers by the Creator. They have continual access to the throne of God (see Job 1:6; 2:1; Rev. 5:11) and are not subject to death.

subjection (v. 8)—In spite of the superiority of angels to humankind, God had originally placed the administration of the earth into the hands of humankind (Gen. 1:26–28). Due to the Fall (Gen. 3), however, humankind has been incapable of fulfilling that divinely ordained position.

glory and honor (v. 9)—Because Jesus "became obedient to the point of death . . . God also has highly exalted Him" (Phil. 2:8, 9). By His redemptive work, Christ has fulfilled all that is required as the supreme representative of humankind. By His incarnation, substitutionary sacrifice, and victory over sin and death (see Rom. 6:23), He has fulfilled man's original purpose. As the Second Adam (1 Cor. 15:47), He was for a short time lower than the angels. Now He has glory and honor, and all things (including angels) are subject to Him.

taste death for everyone (v. 9)—everyone who believes, that is; the death of Christ is efficaciously applied to those who come to God repentantly in faith, asking for saving grace and forgiveness of sins; see 2 Corinthians 5:21; 1 Tim. 2:6; 4:10; Titus 2:11.

fitting (v. 10)—What God did through the humiliation of Jesus Christ was perfectly consistent with His sovereign righteousness and holiness. Without Christ's humiliation and suffering, there could be no redemption. Without redemption, there could be no glorification (see Rom. 8:18, 29–30).

captain (v. 10)—The term is also used in 12:2 and Acts 5:31. It could be translated "pioneer," "leader," or "originator." Christ is the source (see "author" in 5:9, which has the meaning of cause), the initiator, and the leader in regard to salvation. He has led the way into heaven as our forerunner (6:20).

perfect (v. 10)—In His divine nature, Christ was already perfect. However, His human nature was perfected through obedience, including suffering in order that He might be an understanding high priest, an example for believers (see 5:8–9; 7:25–28; Phil. 2:8; 1 Pet. 2:21), and establish the perfect righteousness (Matt. 3:15) to be imputed to believers (2 Corinthians 5:21; Phil. 3:8, 19).

sanctifies (v. 11)—Sanctification sets a person apart for service through purification from sin and conformity to the holiness of God (see 10:10).

My brethren (v. 12)—This is quoted from Psalm 22:22. Jesus had taught that those who do the will of the Father in obedience to His word are His brothers and mother (Matt. 12:50; Luke 8:21). He never directly referred to His disciples by the title of "brethren" until after His resurrection (Matt. 28:10; John 20:17). Not until He had paid the price for their salvation did they truly become His spiritual brothers and sisters. The use of the term demonstrates His full identification with humankind in order to provide complete redemption (Phil. 2:7–9).

partaken . . . shared (v. 14)—The Greek word for "partaken" means fellowship, communion, or partnership. "Shared" means to take hold of something that is not related to one's own kind. The Son of God was not by nature "flesh and blood," but took upon Himself that nature for the sake of providing redemption for humankind.

death . . . power of death (v. 14)—This is the ultimate purpose of the incarnation: Jesus came to earth to die. By dying, He was able to conquer death in His resurrection (John 14:19). By conquering death, He rendered Satan powerless against all who are saved. Satan's use of the power of death is subject to God's will (see Job 2:6).

fear of death (v. 15)—For the believer, "death is swallowed up in victory." Therefore, the fear of death and its spiritual bondage has been brought to an end through the work of Christ.

give aid (v. 16)—The literal meaning is to "take hold of." The sense of "giving aid" is from the picture of taking hold of someone in order to push or pull them to safety, to rescue them. However, there was no thought in Judaism that the Messiah's entrance into the world would be to give aid to the angels. The contrast, using this translation, is weak in comparison with all that has been previously said about Christ's superiority to the angels. The context presents the identification of Christ with humankind in His incarnation—He took upon Himself a human nature (vv. 9–14, 17). When the writer wished to express the concept of giving aid, he chose a different Greek word in verse 18 (also 4:16). Therefore, the translation "take on the nature of" is to be preferred.

seed of Abraham (v. 16)—Christ is that promised seed. Since the readers are Hebrews, they would certainly identify themselves with this description. The Messiah had been born in the line of Abraham in fulfillment of the Old Testament prophecies (Matt. 1:1). One of the chief purposes for the incarnation was the salvation of Israel (Matt. 1:21). Yet another purpose was the fulfillment of the Abrahamic Covenant in regard to the promised seed. Of all peoples, the Hebrews should have been first to recognize the significance and importance of the incarnation.

propitiation (v. 17)—The word means "to conciliate" or "satisfy." Christ's work of propitiation is related to His high priestly ministry. By His partaking a human nature, Christ demonstrated His mercy to humankind and His faithfulness to God by satisfying God's requirement for sin and thus obtaining for His people full forgiveness. (See 1 John 4:10.)

tempted (v. 18)—The genuineness of Christ's humanity is demonstrated by the fact that He was subject to temptation. By experiencing temptation, Jesus became fully capable of understanding and sympathizing with His human brethren (see 4:15). He felt the full force of temptation. Though we often yield to temptation before we feel its full force, Jesus resisted temptation even when the greatest enticement for yielding had become evident.

Understanding the Text

5) What does it mean that God "has in these last days spoken to us by His Son?"

_____

_____

_____

_____

(verses to consider: John 1:1–14)

6) What does it mean that Christ has been appointed heir of all things?

_____

_____

_____

_____

(verses to consider: Ps. 2:8–9; 89:27; Rom. 11:36; Col. 1:15–18)

7) Why did God create angels? What is their role?

_____

_____

_____

_____

(verses to consider: Deut. 33:1–2; Ps. 68:17; 97:7; 104:4; Acts 7:38, 53; Gal. 3:19)

8) What warning does the writer issue to the readers of Hebrews in 2:1–4?

Cross-Reference

Read Colossians 1:13–20.

¹³ *He has delivered us from the power of darkness and conveyed us into the king-dom of the Son of His love,*

¹⁴ *in whom we have redemption through His blood, the forgiveness of sins.*

¹⁵ *He is the image of the invisible God, the firstborn over all creation.*

¹⁶ *For by Him all things were created that are in heaven and that are on earth, visi-ble and invisible, whether thrones or dominions or principalities or powers. All things were created through Him and for Him.*

¹⁷ *And He is before all things, and in Him all things consist.*

¹⁸ *And He is the head of the body, the church, who is the beginning, the firstborn from the dead, that in all things He may have the preeminence.*

¹⁹ *For it pleased the Father that in Him all the fullness should dwell,*

²⁰ *and by Him to reconcile all things to Himself, by Him, whether things on earth or things in heaven, having made peace through the blood of His cross.*

9) In what ways does this great Christological passage echo the themes expressed in Hebrews 1 and 2?

_____

_____

_____

Exploring the Meaning

10) Read Isaiah 61:1–3. How did Jesus Christ fulfill this ancient Messianic prophecy?

_____

_____

(verses to consider: Is. 9:6; Jer. 23:5–6; Luke 4:16–21)

11) Read Psalm 102:25–27. What does this passage suggest about Christ? About the destiny of the universe?

_____

_____

_____

_____

(verses to consider: 2 Pet. 3:10–12; Rev. 6:14)

Summing Up . . .

"Someone has said that Jesus Christ came from the bosom of the Father to the bosom of a woman. He put on humanity that we might put on divinity. He became Son of Man that we might become sons of God. He was born contrary to the laws of nature, lived in poverty, was reared in obscurity, and only once crossed the boundaries of the land in which He was born—and that in His childhood. He had no wealth or influence and had neither training nor education in the world's schools. His relatives were inconspicuous and uninfluential. In infancy He startled a king. In boyhood He puzzled the learned doctors. In manhood He ruled the course of nature. He walked upon the billows and hushed the sea to sleep. He healed the multitudes without medicine and made no charge for His services. He never wrote a book and yet all the libraries of the world could not hold the books about Him. He never wrote a song, yet He has furnished the theme for more songs than all songwriters together. He never founded a college, yet all the schools together cannot boast of as many students as He has. He never practiced medicine and yet He has healed more broken hearts than all the doctors have healed broken bodies. This Jesus Christ is the star of astronomy, the rock of geology, the lion and the lamb of zoology, the harmonizer of all discord, and the healer of all diseases. Throughout history great men have come and gone, yet He lives on. Herod could not kill Him. Satan could not seduce Him. Death could not destroy Him and the grave could not hold Him."—John MacArthur, *Hebrews*, Moody Press, 1983, pp. 9–10.

Reflecting on the Text

12) Given the excellency and supremacy of Christ, why do we still tend to put our trust in other things? In what areas and in what ways do you need to show greater recognition of the fact that Christ is far better than everyone and everything else you might put your trust in?

_____

_____

_____

13) What is the right response to the greatness of Jesus Christ (as portrayed in this passage)?

_____

_____

_____

14) How could you use a non-Christian's preoccupation with angels as an opening for sharing the gospel?

_____

_____

_____

Recording Your Thoughts

For further study, see the following passages:

Numbers 24:14	2 Samuel 7:14	Psalms 2:7, 12; 110:1
Proverbs 30:4	Matthew 22:44	Luke 4:1–13
John 8:12; 14:9	Acts 2:35	Romans 1:4; 3:25
Romans 8:29; 8:34; 15:4	1 Corinthians 10:11, 13	1 Corinthians 15:54
2 Corinthians 4:4, 6	2 Corinthians 12:12	Galatians 3:16
Philippians 2:9–11	Colossians 2:9	2 Timothy 1:9
Titus 2:14	1 Peter 1:10–12; 3:22	1 John 2:2; 4:1
Rev. 5:11; 20:1–5		

Christ: Better than Moses

Opening Thought

1) Take a poll. Ask ten people to name their favorite Old Testament Bible character. Record the results below.

_____

_____

_____

2) What do you know about Moses? Why was and is he so esteemed by the Hebrew people? What would you say were his greatest strengths? His biggest weaknesses? What question would you ask him if given the chance?

_____

_____

_____

3) What are your motives when you give a child, sibling, or friend a sincere warning about a potential danger?

_____

_____

4) How do you tend to react when you are warned about a potential danger? Do you typically respond with disbelief and contempt, or are you usually inclined to heed the words of caution?

_____

_____

Background of the Passage

After having argued for the exalted supremacy of Jesus (who is shown to be superior to the prophets and the angels), the Spirit-led writer of Hebrews makes the case for how Christ is better than Moses, the one through whom the first covenant came.

Moses was honored by the Jews far above any other Jewish human who ever lived. God had miraculously protected him as a baby and personally provided for his burial. Between those two points in his life, history records miracle after miracle. God spoke to Moses face to face, meaning Israel's deliverer had seen the very glory of God and, in fact, even had this glory reflected in his own face for a short time. Revered as the human instrument who led Israel out of Egypt, Moses also brought the Ten Commandments to the people of God. Furthermore, he wrote the entire Pentateuch, which lays out all the laws that governed everything the Jews did. God gave Moses the plans for the Tabernacle and the Ark of the Covenant.

It is not surprising that Moses was so respected by the nation of Israel. Yet, in 3:1–6, the Holy Spirit exhorts Jewish readers to look at Jesus. Moses was indeed great, but Jesus is far superior. In His office, person, and work, Jesus is shown to be superior to Moses. In His office, He is the Apostle and High priest. In His Person, He is the Son of the living God. In His work, He is the Builder of the house.

Verses 7–19 of chapter three contain another warning—a challenge to accept Christ, not just intellectually, but with one's whole heart. Israel's disastrous disbelief in the wilderness is held up as a somber illustration of the consequences of rejecting God's invitation of mercy and grace.

Bible Passage

Read 3:1–19, noting the key words and definitions to the right of the passage.

Hebrews 3:1–19

1 *Therefore, holy brethren, partakers of the heavenly calling, consider the Apostle and High priest of our confession, Christ Jesus,*

2 *who was faithful to Him who appointed Him, as Moses also was faithful in all His house.*

3 *For this One has been counted worthy of more*

holy brethren (v. 1)—The phrase occurs only here and in 1 Thessalonians 5:27, where some manuscripts omit "holy." The writer addresses believers who have a "heavenly calling." They are elsewhere described as desir-

glory than Moses, inasmuch as He who built the house has more honor than the house.

⁴ For every house is built by someone, but He who built all things is God.

⁵ And Moses indeed was faithful in all His house as a servant, for a testimony of those things which would be spoken afterward,

⁶ but Christ as a Son over His own house, whose house we are if we hold fast the confidence and the rejoicing of the hope firm to the end.

⁷ Therefore, as the Holy Spirit says:
"Today, if you will hear His voice,

⁸ Do not harden your hearts as in the rebellion,
In the day of trial in the wilderness,

⁹ Where your fathers tested Me, tried Me,
And saw My works forty years.

¹⁰ Therefore I was angry with that generation,
And said, 'They always go astray in their heart,
And they have not known My ways.'

¹¹ So I swore in My wrath,
'They shall not enter My rest.' "

¹² Beware, brethren, lest there be in any of you an evil heart of unbelief in departing from the living God;

¹³ but exhort one another daily, while it is called "Today," lest any of you be hardened through the deceitfulness of sin.

¹⁴ For we have become partakers of Christ if we hold the beginning of our confidence steadfast to the end,

¹⁵ while it is said:
"Today, if you will hear His voice,
Do not harden your hearts as in the rebellion."

¹⁶ For who, having heard, rebelled? Indeed, was it not all who came out of Egypt, led by Moses?

¹⁷ Now with whom was He angry forty years? Was it not with those who sinned, whose corpses fell in the wilderness?

¹⁸ And to whom did He swear that they would not enter His rest, but to those who did not obey?

¹⁹ So we see that they could not enter in because of unbelief.

ing a "heavenly country" (11:16) and as coming to "the heavenly Jerusalem" (12:22). They are "holy" in the sense that they are set apart unto God and identified with the heavenly realm—citizens of heaven more than citizens of earth.

calling (v. 1)—The reference, as always in the New Testament epistles, is to the effective summons to salvation in Christ.

consider (v. 1)—The writer asks for the readers' complete attention and diligent observation of the superiority of Jesus Christ.

Apostle and High Priest (v.1) —An apostle is a "sent one" who has the rights, power, and authority of the one who sends him. Jesus was sent to earth by the Father (see John 3:17, 34; 5:36–38; 8:42). The topic of the high priesthood of Christ, which was begun in 2:17–18 and is mentioned again here, will be taken up again in greater detail in 4:14–10:18. Meanwhile, the writer presents the superiority of Christ to Moses (vv. 1–6), to Joshua (4:8), and to all other national heroes and Old Testament preachers whom Jews held in high esteem. Jesus Himself spoke of His superiority to Moses in the same context in which He spoke of His being sent by the Father (John 5:36–38, 45–47; see Luke 16:29–31). Moses had been sent by God to deliver His people from historical Egypt and its bondage (Ex. 3:10). Jesus was sent by God to deliver His people from spiritual Egypt and its bondage (2:15).

of our confession (v. 1)— Christ is the center of our confession of faith in the gospel, both in creed and public testimony. The term is used again in 4:14 and 10:23. In all three uses in Hebrews there is a sense of urgency.

Surely, the readers would not give up Christ, whom they had professed, and reject what He had done for them, if they could understand the superiority of His person and work.

house (v. 2)—The term refers to a family of people rather than a building or dwelling (see v. 6; 1 Tim. 3:15). Those who were stewards of a household must above all be faithful. Both Moses (Num. 12:7) and Christ (2:17) faithfully fulfilled their individual, divine appointments to care for the people of God.

He who built (vv. 3–4)—Moses was only a part of God's household of faith, whereas Jesus was the creator of that household (see 2 Sam. 7:13; Zech. 6:12–13; 1 Pet. 2:4–5) and, therefore, is greater than Moses and equal to God.

servant . . . Son (vv. 5–6)—The term for "servant" implies a position of dignity and freedom, not slavery (see Ex. 14:31; Josh. 1:2). However, even as the highest-ranking servant, Moses could never hold the position of Son, which is Christ's alone.

spoken afterward (v. 5)—Moses was faithful primarily as a testimony to that which was to come in Christ (see 11:24–27).

if we hold fast (v. 6)—See verse 14. This is not speaking of how to be saved or remain saved (see 1 Cor. 15:2). It means rather that perseverance in faithfulness is proof of real faith. The one who returns to the rituals of the Levitical system to contribute to his own salvation proves he was never truly part of God's household (see 1 John 2:19), whereas the one who abides in Christ gives evidence of his genuine membership in that household (see Matt. 10:22; Luke 8:15; John 8:31; 15:4–6). The promise of God will fulfill this holding fast (1 Thessalonians 5:24; Jude 24–25).

hope (v. 6)—See the writer's further description of this hope in 6:18–19. This hope rests in Christ Himself, whose redemptive work has accomplished our salvation (Rom. 5:1–2).

Today (v. 7)—The reference is to the present moment while the words of God are fresh in the mind. There is a sense of urgency to immediately give heed to the voice of God. This urgency is emphasized by repeating the reference to "today" from Psalm 95:7 three more times (vv. 13, 15; 4:7) and is the theme of the writer's exposition (see 2 Corinthians 6:2).

My rest (v. 11)—The earthly rest which God promised to give was life in the land of Canaan which Israel would receive as its inheritance (Deut. 12:9–10; Josh. 21:44; 1Kin. 8:56). Because of rebellion against God, an entire generation of the children of Israel was prohibited from entering into that rest in the Promised Land (see Deut. 28:65; Lam. 1:3). The application of this picture is to an individual's spiritual rest in the Lord, which has precedent in the Old Testament (see Ps. 116:7; Is. 28:12). At salvation, every believer enters the true rest, the realm of spiritual promise, never again laboring to achieve through personal effort a righteousness that pleases God. God wanted both kinds of rest for the generation that was delivered from Egypt.

brethren (v. 12)—This admonition is addressed to those having the same potential characteristics as the generation which perished in the wilderness without ever seeing the Land of Promise. They were unbelieving Jewish brethren who were in the company of the "holy brethren" (v. 1). They were admonished to believe and be saved before it was too late. See Introduction: Interpretive Challenges.

an evil heart (v. 12)—all men are born with such a heart (Jer. 17:9); in the case of these Hebrews, that evil manifested itself in disbelief of the gospel, which moved them in the opposite way from God

exhort one another daily (v. 13)—Both individual accountability and corporate responsibility are intended in this admonition. As long as the distressing days were upon them and they were tempted to return to the ineffective Levitical system, they were to encourage one another to identify completely with Jesus Christ.

hardened (v. 13)—Repeated rejection of the gospel concerning Jesus results in a progressive hardening of the heart and will ultimately result in outright antagonism to the gospel. (See 6:4–6; 10:26–29; Acts 19:9.)

deceitfulness (v. 13)—Sin lies and deceives, using every trickery and stratagem possible. The Hebrews deceived themselves with the reasoning that their rejection of Jesus Christ was being faithful to the older system. Their willingness to hang on to the Levitical system was really a rejection of the living Word (4:12) of the "living God" (v. 12), who through Christ had opened up a "new and living way" (10:20). Choosing the path of unbelief always leads only to death (v. 17; 10:26–29; see 2:14–15).

Understanding the Text

5) Why did the writer of Hebrews argue that Jesus is greater than Moses (3:1–6)?

_____

_____

_____

6) What does it mean to be "partakers of the heavenly calling"?

_____

_____

_____

(verses to consider: Eph. 1:3; 2:4–7; Phil. 3:14, 20; Heb. 11:16; 12:22–23)

7) What will be true of those who have truly become "partakers of Christ" (for a hint, see vv. 6 and 14)?

_____

_____

_____

(verses to consider: Matt. 10:22; Luke 8:15; John 8:31; 15:4–6; 1 Thess. 5:24; 1 John 2:19; Jude 24–25)

8) Verses 12–19 feature a warning based on the Old Testament passage quoted in verses 7–11. Who is this warning for? What is the nature of the warning? What will be the result of not heeding this warning?

9) How is sin described in verse 13? What does this mean?

_____

_____

_____

(verses to consider: Rom. 7:11; 2 Thess. 2:10; James 1:14–16)

Cross-Reference

Read Psalm 95.

¹ *Oh come, let us sing to the LORD!*
   Let us shout joyfully to the Rock of our salvation.
² *Let us come before His presence with thanksgiving;*
   Let us shout joyfully to Him with psalms.
³ *For the LORD is the great God,*
   And the great King above all gods.
⁴ *In His hand are the deep places of the earth;*
   The heights of the hills are His also.
⁵ *The sea is His, for He made it;*
   And His hands formed the dry land.
⁶ *Oh come, let us worship and bow down;*
   Let us kneel before the LORD our Maker.
⁷ *For He is our God,*
   And we are the people of His pasture,
   And the sheep of His hand.
   Today, if you will hear His voice:
⁸ *"Do not harden your hearts, as in the rebellion,*
   As in the day of trial in the wilderness,
⁹ *When your fathers tested Me;*
   They tried Me, though they saw My work.
¹⁰ *For forty years I was grieved with that generation,*

And said, 'It is a people who go astray in their hearts,
And they do not know My ways.'
11 *So I swore in My wrath,*
'They shall not enter My rest.' "

10) How were the children of Israel in the wilderness a classic example of unbelief?

_____

_____

_____

Exploring the Meaning

11) Read Proverbs 29:1 and Jude 5. What do these verses say about the consequences of unbelief?

_____

_____

_____

12) Read Ezekiel 33:11. How would you use this verse and Hebrews 3 to demonstrate to a friend that God does not take pleasure in the destruction of unbelievers?

_____

_____

_____

Summing Up . . .

"If we really believe the gospel, if we have committed our life to Jesus Christ, then at the end of the day, the end of the year, the end of life, our commitment will still stand. The greatest proof of salvation is continuance in the Christian life. The true believer stays with Christ. . . . When someone departs from the gospel, backs away from the faith, we can only conclude that this person never believed. . . . Staying with the Lord marks the difference between possession and profession."—John MacArthur, *Hebrews*, Moody Press, 1983, pp. 93–94.

Reflecting on the Text

13) The passage urges us to "consider. . . Christ Jesus." What would this look like in your everyday life? What are some evidences that a person is, in fact, keeping his or her eyes on the Savior?

_____

_____

(verses to consider: Phil. 3:8–14; Heb. 12:1–2)

14) What works of God (see 3:9) in your life should prompt a deeper and more consistent daily walk of faith?

_____

_____

15) Hebrews 3:13 issues the command to exhort one another to identify with Christ rather than be overcome by unbelief. How can God use you today to help an unbelieving person trust in Christ?

_____

_____

Recording Your Thoughts

For further study, see the following passages:

Exodus 17:12; 33:11	Numbers 14:22–23	Joshua 8:31
1 Kings 2:3	Psalm 95:7–11	Luke 2:22; 16:31
John 5:46; 8:35; 14:16	Acts 13:39	Romans 7:11; 8:30
1 Corinthians 4:2; 7:21	2 Corinthians 9:13	Ephesians 2:19–22
1 Timothy 3:15; 6:12	Hebrews 6:6	1 Peter 1:3; 2:5; 4:17

A Better Rest

Opening Thought

1) What is the most restful place you've ever been? What made it such a serene location?

_____

_____

_____

2) How would you define or describe the rest that God offers?

_____

_____

_____

3) Augustine once said, "You have made us for Yourself, O God, and our hearts are restless until they find rest in Thee." What do you think he meant by this statement?

_____

_____

_____

4) What sort of things keep people from experiencing God's perfect rest?

_____

_____

_____

Background of the Passage

The English *rest* and the Greek word that it translates in chapter 4 have similar meanings. The basic idea is that of ceasing from work or from any kind of action. You stop doing what you are doing. Action, labor, or exertion is over. Applied to God's rest, it means no more self-effort as far as salvation is concerned. It means the end of trying to please God by our feeble, fleshly works. God's perfect rest is a rest in free grace.

Rest further means freedom from whatever worries or disturbs you. It means freedom from guilt over sin. It means no more shifting about in frustration from one thing to another, no more running in circles. It means remaining confident, keeping trust. To enter into God's rest means that for the remainder of our lives and for all eternity we can lean on God. Such rest is full, blessed, sweet, satisfying, peaceful. Amazingly, this is what God offers every person in Christ.

Chapter 4 continues the warning to informed but unresponsive Jews that began in 3:7. These Jews not only knew the basic truths of the gospel but had even renounced Judaism. Still, however, they did not trust in Christ. This warning, of course, applies to anyone who is hesitating to commit himself fully to Jesus Christ. It can be summarized: "Do not harden your hearts like Israel did in the wilderness." Though the Israelites had left Egypt, they often longed to go back. They stubbornly refused to trust the Lord completely. The old way of life, oppressive and disappointing as it was, still had an alluring appeal. So these Jews halted at the critical moment of decision. This is why they were not allowed to enter the Promised Land and into God's rest. This is precisely what happens still to many who are drawn to Jesus Christ. Unbelief causes one to forfeit the possibility of rest—that is the writer's thought.

Bible Passage

Read 4:1–13, noting the key words and definitions to the right of the passage.

Hebrews 4:1–13

¹ *Therefore, since a promise remains of entering His rest, let us fear lest any of you seem to have come short of it.*

² *For indeed the gospel was preached to us as well*

promise (v. 1)—This is the first use of this important word in Hebrews. The content of this promise is defined as "entering His rest."

His rest (v. 1)—This is the rest

as to them; but the word which they heard did not profit them, not being mixed with faith in those who heard it.

3 For we who have believed do enter that rest, as He has said:
"So I swore in My wrath,
'They shall not enter My rest,' "
although the works were finished from the foundation of the world.

4 For He has spoken in a certain place of the seventh day in this way: "And God rested on the seventh day from all His works";

5 and again in this place: "They shall not enter My rest."

6 Since therefore it remains that some must enter it, and those to whom it was first preached did not enter because of disobedience,

7 again He designates a certain day, saying in David, "Today," after such a long time, as it has been said:
"Today, if you will hear His voice,
Do not harden your hearts."

8 For if Joshua had given them rest, then He would not afterward have spoken of another day.

9 There remains therefore a rest for the people of God.

10 For he who has entered His rest has himself also ceased from his works as God did from His.

11 Let us therefore be diligent to enter that rest, lest anyone fall according to the same example of disobedience.

12 For the word of God is living and powerful, and sharper than any two-edged sword, piercing even to the division of soul and spirit, and of joints and marrow, and is a discerner of the thoughts and intents of the heart.

13 And there is no creature hidden from His sight, but all things are naked and open to the eyes of Him to whom we must give account.

which God gives, therefore it is called "My rest" (Ps. 95:11) and "His rest." For believers, God's rest includes His peace, confidence of salvation, reliance on His strength, and assurance of a future heavenly home.

come short (v. 1)—The entire phrase could be translated "lest you think you have come too late to enter into the rest of God" (see 12:15). With reverential fear all are to examine their own spiritual condition and to actively press for commitment on the part of others.

faith (v. 2)—Mere knowledge of God's message is not sufficient. It must be appropriated by saving faith. Later in the epistle a much longer exposition will take up this topic of faith (10:19–12:29). The writer's point of comparison is that, like the Jews who left Egypt (3:16–19), his generation had also received God's message through the preaching of the gospel—they had been evangelized.

we . . . do enter (v. 3)—Those who exercise faith in the message of God will enter into their spiritual rest. This is the corollary of Psalm 95:11 which states the opposite side: that the unbeliever will not enter into the rest which God provides.

finished from the foundation of the world (v. 3)—The spiritual rest which God gives is not something incomplete or unfinished. It is a rest which is based upon a finished work which God purposed in eternity past, just like the rest which God took after He finished creation (v. 4).

He has spoken . . . of the seventh day in this way (v. 4) —By way of explanation for the statement in verse 3, the writer cites the illustration of the seventh day of creation. Then he repeats the last part of Psalm 95:11.

29

some must enter it (vv. 6–7)—The opportunity to enter God's rest remains open (see "a promise remains" in v. 1). It is not yet too late. God had offered the rest to His people in Moses' time and continued to offer it in David's time. He is still patiently inviting His people to enter His rest. Quoting Psalm 95:7–8 once again (see 3:7, 15), the author urges an immediate, positive response. The themes of urgency and obedience are thus combined in a clear invitation to the readers.

if Joshua had given them rest (vv. 8–10)—God's true rest did not come through Joshua or Moses, but through Jesus Christ, who is greater than either one. Joshua led the nation of Israel into the land of their promised rest (see the note on 3:11). However, that was merely the earthly rest which was but the shadow of what was involved in the heavenly rest. The very fact that, according to Psalm 95, God was still offering His rest in the time of David (long after Israel had been in the Land) meant that the rest being offered was spiritual—superior to that which Joshua obtained. Israel's earthly rest was disturbed by the attacks of enemies and the daily cycle of work. The heavenly rest is characterized by the fullness of heavenly promise (Eph. 1:3) and the absence of any labor to obtain it.

rest (v. 9)—A different Greek word for "rest" meaning "Sabbath rest" is introduced here, and this is its only appearance in the New Testament. The writer chose the word to draw the readers' attention back to the "seventh day" mentioned in verse 4 and to set up the explanation in verse 10 ("ceased from his works as God did from His").

Let us . . . be diligent (vv. 11–13)—The concluding third part of the exposition of Psalm 95:7–11 emphasizes the accountability which comes to those who have heard the Word of God. Scripture records the examples of those in the wilderness with Moses, those who entered Canaan with Joshua, and those who received the same opportunity in David's day. It is the Word which must be believed and obeyed and the Word which will judge the disobedient.

two-edged sword (v. 12)—While the Word of God is comforting and nourishing to those who believe, it is a tool of judgment and execution for those who have not committed themselves to Jesus Christ. Some of the Hebrews were merely going through the motions of belonging to Christ. Intellectually, they were at least partly persuaded, but inside they were not committed to Him. God's Word would expose their shallow beliefs and even their false intentions.

division of soul and spirit (v. 12)—These terms do not describe two separate entities (any more than "thoughts and intents" do) but are used as one might say "heart and soul" to express fullness. Elsewhere these two terms are used interchangeably to describe man's immaterial self, his eternal inner person.

open to the eyes of Him (v. 13)—"Open" is a specialized term used just this one time in the New Testament. It originally meant to expose the neck either in preparation for sacrifice or for beheading. Perhaps the use of "sword" in the previous verse triggered the term. Each individual is judged not only by the Word of God (see John 12:48) but by God Himself. We are accountable to the living, written Word and to the living God who is its author.

Understanding the Text

5) Is the rest described in chapter 4 only physical and national in the land of Canaan? Or is it something more? Explain your answer based on the passage.

_____

_____

_____

_____

_____

6) Who, according to this chapter, gets to experience God's rest?

_____

_____

_____

_____

7) To what does the Spirit-guided writer compare God's Word? What role does the Word of God play in the life of the believer and the unbeliever?

_____

_____

_____

(verses to consider: 1 Sam. 16:7; 2 Tim. 3:16–17)

Cross-Reference

Read 1 Corinthians 10:5–13.

5 *But with most of them God was not well pleased, for their bodies were scattered in the wilderness.*

6 *Now these things became our examples, to the intent that we should not lust after evil things as they also lusted.*

7 *And do not become idolaters as were some of them. As it is written, "The people sat down to eat and drink, and rose up to play."*

8 *Nor let us commit sexual immorality, as some of them did, and in one day twenty-three thousand fell;*

9 *nor let us tempt Christ, as some of them also tempted, and were destroyed by serpents;*

10 *nor complain, as some of them also complained, and were destroyed by the destroyer.*

11 *Now all these things happened to them as examples, and they were written for our admonition, upon whom the ends of the ages have come.*

12 *Therefore let him who thinks he stands take heed lest he fall.*

13 *No temptation has overtaken you except such as is common to man; but God is faithful, who will not allow you to be tempted beyond what you are able, but with the temptation will also make the way of escape, that you may be able to bear it.*

8) How can we learn from the poor choices of the Israelites (and God's judgment of them)?

_____

_____

_____

_____

_____

Exploring the Meaning

9) Read Joshua 21:43–45. What historical background regarding Joshua and the ancient Israelites does this passage provide? From what you know of Old Testament history, how long did this rest last? How does this compare to the spiritual rest that the writer of Hebrews encourages us to enter?

_____

_____

_____

_____

_____

10) Read Galatians 2:16. How does experiencing God's rest depend on personal faith?

_____

_____

_____

_____

_____

(verses to consider: Matt. 7:21–23; Luke 13:25–28; Rom. 2:29; 1 Thess. 2:13)

Summing Up . . .

"The need for God's rest is urgent. A person should diligently, with intense purpose and concern, secure it. It is not that he can work his way to salvation, but that he should diligently seek to enter God's rest by faith—lest he, like the Israelites in the wilderness, lose the opportunity. God cannot be trifled with."—John MacArthur, *Hebrews*, Moody Press, 1983, p. 105.

Reflecting on the Text

11) Take some time to examine your own heart and life. Have you entered into God's rest through faith? Or are you still trying to be saved through your own work and self-effort? What evidence would you give to support your answer?

_____

_____

_____

_____

_____

12) Think of someone you know who has heard the message of the gospel but has not yet entered God's rest. How can you encourage him or her to trust fully in Jesus Christ? What examples from God's Word could you point to as you urge him or her to take this step?

_____

_____

_____

_____

_____

13) In addition to the negative example of the ancient Israelites, what other mistakes (made by others) can you learn from this week?

_____

_____

_____

_____

Recording Your Thoughts

_____

_____

_____

_____

_____

_____

_____

_____

_____

_____

For further study, see the following passages:

Genesis 2:2	Psalm 95	Luke 10:27
John 6:63, 68	Acts 4:32; 7:38	Romans 10:21
1 Thessalonians 5:23		

Our Great High priest

Opening Thought

1) Who are the three most understanding and sympathetic people in your life? What do you think makes them so caring and encouraging?

_____

_____

_____

_____

_____

2) Rank the following items from 1 (most) to 7 (least) in terms of how important they are to being an effective spiritual leader:

_____ vision

_____ compassion

_____ communication skills

_____ experience

_____ courage

_____ approachability

_____ good looks

3) When is the last time you "went to bat" for someone else in trouble? What happened?

_____

_____

_____

_____

Background of the Passage

Many people have a distorted picture of Christianity, as having no message but "fire and brimstone, hell and damnation." Anyone who read only the first four chapters of Hebrews might be confirmed in such thinking. For until now the subject matter of the epistle to the Hebrews has been largely negative: Unbelievers will be doomed—forever apart from God and His perfect rest. God's Word, likened to a two-edged sword (4:12), has been shown in its all-seeing and judgmental role.

Beginning in 4:14, however, the focus turns to the positive side of the gospel. Salvation does more, immeasurably more, than merely keep sinners out of hell.

Salvation not only delivers from spiritual death, it produces spiritual life. It should be sought not only because of the terrible consequences of rejecting it but also because of what we gain when we embrace it. It's true that we receive Jesus Christ and enter into God's rest to escape judgment and wrath at the hands of the righteous Judge of the universe. But we also enter into God's rest because of the beauty and grace of our merciful High priest.

The heart of the Book of Hebrews focuses on the high priesthood of Jesus. It is a superior priesthood that, more than anything else, makes the New Covenant superior to the Old. He alone has done what all the priests together of the old order did not do and could never have done. In one perfect and final act of sacrifice, He opened the way to God permanently. As a result, anyone at any time may, by faith in Christ, enter into God's presence.

Bible Passage

Read 4:14–5:10, noting the key words and definitions to the right of the passage.

Hebrews 4:14–5:10

¹⁴ *Seeing then that we have a great High priest who has passed through the heavens, Jesus the Son of God, let us hold fast our confession.*

¹⁵ *For we do not have a High priest who cannot sympathize with our weaknesses, but was in all points tempted as we are, yet without sin.*

passed through the heavens
(v. 14)—Just as the high priest under the Old Covenant passed through three areas (the outer court, the Holy Place, and the Most Holy Place) to make the atoning sacrifice, Jesus passed through three heavens (the atmospheric heaven, the stellar heaven, and God's abode;

¹⁶ *Let us therefore come boldly to the throne of grace, that we may obtain mercy and find grace to help in time of need.*

^{5:1} *For every high priest taken from among men is appointed for men in things pertaining to God, that he may offer both gifts and sacrifices for sins.*

² *He can have compassion on those who are ignorant and going astray, since he himself is also subject to weakness.*

³ *Because of this he is required as for the people, so also for himself, to offer sacrifices for sins.*

⁴ *And no man takes this honor to himself, but he who is called by God, just as Aaron was.*

⁵ *So also Christ did not glorify Himself to become High priest, but it was He who said to Him:*
"You are My Son,
Today I have begotten You."

⁶ *As He also says in another place:*
"You are a priest forever
According to the order of Melchizedek";

⁷ *who, in the days of His flesh, when He had offered up prayers and supplications, with vehement cries and tears to Him who was able to save Him from death, and was heard because of His godly fear,*

⁸ *though He was a Son, yet He learned obedience by the things which He suffered.*

⁹ *And having been perfected, He became the author of eternal salvation to all who obey Him,*

¹⁰ *called by God as High priest "according to the order of Melchizedek,"*

see 2 Corinthians 12:2–4) after making the perfect, final sacrifice. Once a year on the Day of Atonement the High priest of Israel would enter the Most Holy Place to make atonement for the sins of the people (Lev. 16). That tabernacle was but a limited copy of the heavenly reality (see 8:1–5). When Jesus entered into the heavenly Most Holy Place, having accomplished redemption, the earthly facsimile was replaced by the reality of heaven itself. Freed from that which is earthly, the Christian faith is characterized by the heavenly.

Jesus the Son of God (v. 14) —The use of both the title of humanity (Jesus) and of deity (Son of God) is significant. One of the few cases of such a juxtaposition is in 1 John 1:7, where His sacrifice for sins is emphasized.

hold fast our confession (v. 14)—See the notes on 3:1, 6; 10:23.

all points tempted (v. 15)— See the notes on 2:17–18. The writer here adds to his statements in 2:18 that Jesus was sinless. He was able to be tempted (Matt. 4:1–11), but not able to sin (see the notes on 7:26).

come boldly to the throne of grace (v. 16)—Most ancient rulers were unapproachable by anyone but their high est advisers (see Esth. 4:11). In contrast, the Holy Spirit calls for all to come confidently before God's throne to receive mercy and grace through Jesus Christ (see 7:25; 10:22; see Introduction: Historical and Theological Themes). The ark of the covenant was viewed as the place on earth where God sat enthroned between the cherubim (see 2 Kin. 19:15; Jer. 3:16–17). Oriental thrones included a footstool—yet another metaphor for the ark (see Ps. 132:7). It was at the throne of God that Christ made atonement for sins, and it is there that grace is dispensed to believers for all the issues of life. "Grace to you" became a standard greeting among believers who celebrated this provision (Rom. 1:7; 16:20, 24; 1 Cor. 1:3; 16:23; 2 Corinthians 1:2; 13:14; Gal. 1:3; 6:18; Eph. 1:2; 6:24; Phil. 1:2; 4:18; Col. 1:2; 4:18; 1 Thess. 1:1; 5:28; 2 Thess. 1:2; 3:18; 1 Tim. 1:2; 6:21; 2 Tim. 1:2; 4:22; Titus 1:4; 3:15; Philem. 3:25).

to help in time of need (v. 16)—See the notes on 2:16, 18.

high priest taken from among men (v. 5:1)—No angel with supernatural power could serve as high priest. Only men with the weaknesses of humanity could serve as high priest (v. 2; 7:28). The position of high priest in the Levitical system was by appointment only. No man could legitimately appoint himself high priest. The use of the present tense in these verses would seem to indicate that the Levitical system still was being practiced at the time of this epistle (see Introduction: Author and Date).

gifts and sacrifices (v. 1)—The first term might refer especially to the grain offerings under the Old Covenant, which were for thanksgiving or dedication. That would leave the second term to refer to blood offerings for the expiation of sins (see Lev. 1–5). However, "gifts" is used in 8:4 to refer to all of the various sacrifices (see 8:3). The three occurrences of the phrase in the New Testament (see 8:3; 9:9) employ a Greek construction which expresses a closer relationship between the two terms than is normally indicated by the word "and." This could indicate that no distinction should be made between the terms, and that "for sins" should be taken with both.

have compassion (v. 2)—This verb occurs only here in the New Testament. It carries the idea of maintaining a controlled but gentle attitude in the treatment of those who are spiritually ignorant and wayward. Impatience, loathing, and indignation have no part in priestly ministry. Such moderation and gentleness come from realizing one's own human frailty. The priest would be reminded of his own sinful humanity every time he offered sacrifices for his own sins (v. 3).

called by God (v. 4)—A high priest was selected and called by God into service (see Ex. 28; Num. 16:1–40; 1 Sam. 16:1–3).

Melchizedek (v. 6)—As king of Salem and priest of the Most High God in the time of Abraham, he was also a king-priest (Gen. 14:18–20). The Melchizedekan priesthood is discussed in detail in chapter 7.

who (v. 7)—The subsequent context makes it clear that this refers back to Christ, the main subject in verse 5. In Gethsemane, Jesus agonized and wept, but committed Himself to do the Father's will in accepting the cup of suffering which would bring His death (Luke 22:44–45). Anticipating bearing the burden of judgment for sin, Jesus felt its fullest pain and grief. Though He bore the penalty in silence and did not seek to deliver Himself from it (Is. 53:7), He did cry out from the agony of the fury of God's wrath poured on His perfectly holy and obedient person. Jesus asked to be saved from remaining in death, i.e., to be resurrected (see Ps. 16:9–10).

learned obedience (v. 8)—Christ did not need to suffer in order to conquer or correct any disobedience. In His deity (as the Son of God), He understood obedience completely. As the incarnate Lord, He humbled Himself to learn (see Luke 2:52). He learned obedience for the same reasons He bore temptation: to confirm His humanity and experience its sufferings to the fullest (see the notes on 2:10; Phil. 2:8). Christ's obedience was also necessary so that He could fulfill all righteousness and thus prove to be the perfect sacrifice to take the place of sinners (1 Pet. 3:18). He was the perfectly righteous One, whose righteousness would be imputed to sinners.

perfected . . . author of eternal salvation (v. 9)—See the notes on 2:10. Because of the perfect righteousness of Jesus Christ and His perfect sacrifice for sin, He became the cause of salvation.

obey Him (v. 9)—True salvation evidences itself in obedience to Christ, from the initial obedience to the gospel command to repent and believe (see Acts 5:32; Rom. 1:5; 2 Thess. 1:8; 1 Pet. 1:2, 22; 4:17) to a life pattern of obedience to the Word.

Understanding the Text

4) How is Jesus able to sympathize with "our weaknesses"?

_____

_____

_____

5) In light of what Christ has done for us as the great High Priest, how are we encouraged to approach God?

_____

_____

_____

(verses to consider: 2 Corinthians 4:15; 9:8; 12:9; Eph. 1:7; 2:7)

6) How did Christ's suffering and sacrifice for men show Him to be the perfect High priest?

_____

_____

_____

7) How and why did the writer of Hebrews compare Jesus to Melchizedek?

_____

_____

_____

(verses to consider: Gen. 14:18–20; Hebrews 7:1–3)

Cross-Reference

Read Psalm 110.

A Psalm of David.
1 *The LORD said to my Lord,*
"Sit at My right hand,
Till I make Your enemies Your footstool."
2 *The LORD shall send the rod of Your strength out of Zion.*
Rule in the midst of Your enemies!
3 *Your people shall be volunteers*
In the day of Your power;
In the beauties of holiness, from the womb of the morning,
You have the dew of Your youth.
4 *The LORD has sworn*
And will not relent,
"You are a priest forever
According to the order of Melchizedek."
5 *The LORD is at Your right hand;*
He shall execute kings in the day of His wrath.
6 *He shall judge among the nations,*
He shall fill the places with dead bodies,
He shall execute the heads of many countries.
7 *He shall drink of the brook by the wayside;*
Therefore He shall lift up the head.

8) How does this Old Testament passage speak of Messiah?

_____

_____

_____

Exploring the Meaning

9) Read Leviticus 16:1–34. What five words would you use to describe the ancient Jewish sacrificial system? How did Christ render these practices obsolete?

_____

_____

_____

10) Read Isaiah 53:1–12. What does this ancient prophecy say about Christ's work on behalf of sinners?

_____

_____

_____

(verses to consider: John 17:4–5; Rom. 3:23–26)

11) Read 1 Peter 2:5, 9. What does the apostle mean when he says that Christians are a "holy priesthood"?

_____

_____

_____

Summing Up . . .

"In sending His Son, Jesus Christ, God no longer kept Himself aloof, transcendent, and separate from men. He entered into the human world and felt everything that men will ever feel in order that He might be a sympathetic, merciful, and faithful High priest. If God had never become man, He never could have been a high priest, a mediator, or an intercessor. He never could have offered the perfect and absolute sacrifice for the sins of His people, which divine justice required. The incarnation was not an option; it was an absolute necessity. It was an imperative if men were to be saved. . . . God had to come down to where we are in order to pick us up and bring us back to Himself."—John MacArthur, _Hebrews_, Moody Press, 1983, pp. 119–120.

Reflecting on the Text

12) In what specific area of your life do you sense a special need to "approach the throne of grace"? How, based on this passage, do you anticipate being received?

_____

_____

_____

13) As a perfect High priest, how does Christ deserve your honor today? How specifically will you live with gratitude and reverence?

_____

_____

_____

14) When we have sinned and are in trouble, or are dealing with the temptation to sin, we often hesitate to turn to God. We either think we can handle it on our own, or we feel the need to "clean up our act" before we approach Him. How can Christ's understanding and sympathetic nature motivate you to turn to Him today in times of temptation and trouble?

_____

_____

_____

Recording Your Thoughts

_____

_____

_____

_____

_____

_____

For further study, see the following passages:

Leviticus 16	Numbers 16	Psalm 2:7
Matthew 5:13	Luke 2:52	Romans 6:16
Ephesians 1:3	Philippians 3:20	Colossians 1:5
1 Thessalonians 1:10	1 Peter 1:4	1 John 4:15; 5:5

Full Commitment to Christ

Opening Thought

1) List five common traits of a person who is considered
• physically immature

_____

_____

• emotionally immature

_____

_____

• spiritually immature

_____

_____

2) When was the last time you failed to keep a promise? What happened?

_____

_____

_____

3) How can a Christian have assurance of his or her salvation?

_____

_____

_____

Background of the Passage

Contrary to what many believe, the epistle to the Hebrews does not contrast two kinds of Christianity. It does not distinguish immature Christians from mature ones. The writer, under the inspiration of the Holy Spirit, is delineating the differences between Judaism and Christianity, between the unsaved Jew in Judaism and the redeemed Jew in Christianity.

In this hotly debated and much-disputed section of Hebrews, the writer addresses the issue of spiritual maturity. He speaks to unbelievers first (5:11–6:8), warning them of the grave dangers of rejecting God's revelation and grace. The warning in this passage is directed to the same group as are the first two (2:1–4; 3:7–19)—to unbelieving Jews who knew much about the gospel but who had not gone so far as to embrace it personally. Some probably had made a shallow profession of faith without actually believing. They are told of the danger of not entering into the blessing of the New Covenant, apart from which they cannot have eternal life. They are so close, yet so far away from true salvation.

Next, the text addresses genuine believers (6:9–20), reminding them of the certainties of God's promises. The divine assurance is that all who come to Him through His Son will be saved. God has never reneged on one of His promises, and He never will. He cannot possibly be unfaithful. Thus, it is impossible for anyone who trusts in Christ not to be saved or to lose salvation once it is attained. How freeing to know that we can trust God because He has no capacity for deception or failure in His nature! This the wonderfully reassuring truth for those who have believed the gospel.

Bible Passage

Read 5:11–6:20, noting the key words and definitions to the right of the passage.

Hebrews 5:11–6:20

11 *of whom we have much to say, and hard to explain, since you have become dull of hearing.*
12 *For though by this time you ought to be teachers, you need someone to teach you again the first principles of the oracles of God; and you have come to need milk and not solid food.*

of whom (v. 11)—An alternate translation would be "of which" (meaning the relationship of Christ's high priesthood to that of Melchizedek). Logically and stylistically, verse 11 appears to introduce the entire section from 5:11 to 6:12. The same Greek verb "become" forms brackets around the section: "become dull" (v. 11) and "become sluggish" (6:12).

¹³ *For everyone who partakes only of milk is unskilled in the word of righteousness, for he is a babe.*

¹⁴ *But solid food belongs to those who are of full age, that is, those who by reason of use have their senses exercised to discern both good and evil.*

^{6:1} *Therefore, leaving the discussion of the elementary principles of Christ, let us go on to perfection, not laying again the foundation of repentance from dead works and of faith toward God,*

² *of the doctrine of baptisms, of laying on of hands, of resurrection of the dead, and of eternal judgment.*

³ *And this we will do if God permits.*

⁴ *For it is impossible for those who were once enlightened, and have tasted the heavenly gift, and have become partakers of the Holy Spirit,*

⁵ *and have tasted the good word of God and the powers of the age to come,*

⁶ *if they fall away, to renew them again to repentance, since they crucify again for themselves the Son of God, and put Him to an open shame.*

⁷ *For the earth which drinks in the rain that often comes upon it, and bears herbs useful for those by whom it is cultivated, receives blessing from God;*

⁸ *but if it bears thorns and briars, it is rejected and near to being cursed, whose end is to be burned.*

⁹ *But, beloved, we are confident of better things concerning you, yes, things that accompany salvation, though we speak in this manner.*

¹⁰ *For God is not unjust to forget your work and labor of love which you have shown toward His name, in that you have ministered to the saints, and do minister.*

¹¹ *And we desire that each one of you show the same diligence to the full assurance of hope until the end,*

dull (v. 11)—The Hebrews' spiritual lethargy and slow response to gospel teaching prevented additional teaching at this time. This is a reminder that failure to appropriate the truth of the gospel produces stagnation in spiritual advancement and the inability to understand or assimilate additional teaching. Such a situation exists also among the Gentiles who have received revelatory truth (natural or general revelation) from God in the creation (Rom. 1:18–20). Rejection of that revelation results in a process of hardening (Rom. 1:21–32). The Hebrews had not only received the same general revelation, but they had also received special revelation consisting of the Old Testament Scriptures, the Messiah Himself, and the teaching of the apostles (2:3–4). Until the Hebrews obeyed the revelation they had received and obtained eternal salvation (v. 8), additional teaching about the Messiah's Melchizedekan priesthood would be of no profit to them.

teachers (v. 12)—Every believer is to be a teacher (see Deut. 6:7). If these Hebrews had really obeyed the gospel of Christ, they would have been passing that message on to others. The Jews were instructed in the law and prided themselves because they taught the law, but had not really understood or appropriated its truths to themselves.

oracles (v. 12)—These are contained in the Old Testament Scripture, which had laid the foundation for the gospel and had been committed into the care of the Hebrews. The ABCs of the law tutored the Hebrews in order to lead them to faith in the Messiah. They had also heard the New Testament gospel (2:2–4).

milk (vv. 12–13)—Knowledge without obedience does not advance a person. In fact, by rejecting saving faith, the Hebrews were regressing in their understanding concerning the Messiah. They had long enough been exposed to the gospel to be

¹² *that you do not become sluggish, but imitate those who through faith and patience inherit the promises.*

¹³ *For when God made a promise to Abraham, because He could swear by no one greater, He swore by Himself,*

¹⁴ *saying, "Surely blessing I will bless you, and multiplying I will multiply you."*

¹⁵ *And so, after he had patiently endured, he obtained the promise.*

¹⁶ *For men indeed swear by the greater, and an oath for confirmation is for them an end of all dispute.*

¹⁷ *Thus God, determining to show more abundantly to the heirs of promise the immutability of His counsel, confirmed it by an oath,*

¹⁸ *that by two immutable things, in which it is impossible for God to lie, we might have strong consolation, who have fled for refuge to lay hold of the hope set before us.*

¹⁹ *This hope we have as an anchor of the soul, both sure and steadfast, and which enters the Presence behind the veil,*

²⁰ *where the forerunner has entered for us, even Jesus, having become High priest forever according to the order of Melchizedek.*

teaching it to others, but were babies, too infantile and unskilled to comprehend, let alone teach, the truth of God.

word of righteousness (v. 13) —This is the message about the righteousness of Christ which we have by faith (Rom. 3:21–22; 1 Cor. 1:30; 2 Corinthians 5:21). The phrase is equivalent to the gospel of salvation by faith rather than works.

of full age (v. 14)—The same Greek root is translated "perfection" in 6:1 and is elsewhere translated "perfect" (7:11, 19, 28; 9:9; 10:1, 14; 11:40; 12:23). It is used in Hebrews, including this text, as a synonym for salvation. In that sense it refers to the completion which comes when one becomes a believer in Christ, rather than referring to Christian who has become mature, as is typical Pauline usage (see Col. 4:12). Jesus invited unbelieving Jews to the salvation perfection which came only through following Him in faith (Matt. 19:21). Paul wrote that those who had come to Christ by faith were thereby mature and able to receive the wisdom of God. He described believers as "mature" when he referred to those whose righteousness was in Christ (Phil. 3:2–20), as opposed to those who had confidence in the flesh. Paul also declared that the apostles warned and taught everyone "that we may present every man perfect in Christ Jesus" (Col. 1:28).

exercised (v. 14)—The deeper, more "solid" truths about the priesthood of the Lord Jesus could only be given to those who knew Him as Savior. Athletic training and competition form the metaphor implied by this particular word (see 1 Tim. 4:7–8). The one who has come to Christ for spiritual completion is the trained by the Word to discern truth from error and holy behavior from unholy.

leaving (v. 6:1)—This "leaving" does not mean to despise or abandon the basic doctrines. They are the place to start, not stop. They are the gate of entrance on the road to salvation in Christ.

elementary principles of Christ (v. 1)—As "the oracles of God" in 5:12 refers to the Old Testament, so does this phrase. The writer is referring to basic Old Testament teaching that prepared the way for Messiah—the beginning teaching about Christ. These Old Testament "principles" include the six features listed in verses 1–2.

go on to perfection (v. 1)—This refers to salvation by faith in Messiah Jesus. See the note on 5:14. The verb is passive, so as to indicate "let us be carried to salvation." That is not a matter of learners being carried by teachers, but both being carried forward by God. The writer warns his Jewish readers that there is no value in stopping with the Old Testament basics and repeating ("laying again") what was only intended to be foundational.

repentance from dead works (v. 1)—This Old Testament form of repentance is the turning away from evil deeds that bring death (see Ezek. 18:4; Rom. 6:23) and turning to God. Too often the Jew turned to God only in a superficial fashion—fulfilling the letter of the law as evidence of his repentance. The inner man was still dead (Matt. 23:25–28; Rom. 2:28–29). Such repentance was not the kind which brought salvation (v. 6; 12:17; see Acts 11:18; 2 Corinthians 7:10). Under the New Covenant, however, "repentance toward God" is coupled with "faith in our Lord Jesus Christ" (Acts 20:21). Christ's atoning sacrifice saves from "dead works" (9:14; see John 14:6).

faith toward God (v. 1)—Faith directed only toward the Father is unacceptable without faith in His Son, Jesus Christ (see James 2:14–20).

baptisms (v. 2)—A better translation would be "washings" as in 9:10. The plural Greek term is never used of Christian baptism and is inconsistent with the singular concept of Christian baptism. In the Old Testament Levitical system, there were many ceremonial cleansings, which were outward signs of heart cleansing (see Ex. 30:18–21; Lev. 16:4, 24, 26, 28; Mark 7:4, 8). The New Covenant called for an inner washing (Titus 3:5) that regenerated the soul.

laying on of hands (v. 2)—Under the Old Covenant, the person who brought a sacrifice placed his hands on it to symbolize his identification with it as a substitute sacrifice for sin (Lev. 1:4; 3:8, 13; 16:21). There could also be a reference here to solemn priestly blessings (see Matt. 19:13).

resurrection . . . and of eternal judgment (v. 2)—The Pharisees believed in the resurrection from the dead (Acts 23:8) but were still spiritually dead (Matt. 23:27). They also believed in the judgment of God and were headed for it. It is significant that all of the doctrines listed in verses 1 and 2 can be associated with the Pharisees, who were attracted to and sometimes associated with Jesus (Luke 7:36–50; 13:31; 14:1; John 3:1). Paul was a Pharisee before his conversion (Phil. 3:5). The Pharisees were products of the pursuit of righteousness by works of the law rather than by faith (Rom. 9:30–32; 10:1–3). A portion of the Hebrews to whom this epistle was written may have been Pharisees.

we will do (v. 3)—The writer is likely both giving his own testimony about going on from Old Testament teaching to embrace the New Covenant in Jesus Christ and also identifying himself with the readers. Salvation always requires God's enablement (see John 6:44).

enlightened (v. 4)—They had received instruction in biblical truth which was accompanied by intellectual perception. Understanding the gospel is not the equivalent of regeneration (see 10:26, 32). In John 1:9 it is clear that enlightening is not the equivalent of salvation. (See 10:29.)

tasted the heavenly gift (v. 4)—Tasting in the figurative sense in the New Testament refers to consciously experiencing something (see 2:9). The experience might be momentary or continuing. Christ's "tasting" of death (2:9) was obviously momentary and not continuing or permanent. All men experience the goodness of God, but that does not mean they are all saved (see Matt. 5:45). Many Jews during the Lord's earthly ministry experienced the blessings from heaven He brought—in healings and deliverance from demons, as well as eating the food He miraculously created. Whether the gift refers to Christ (see John 6:51; 2 Corinthians 9:15) or to the Holy Spirit (see Acts 2:38; 1 Pet. 1:12), experiencing either one was not the equivalent of salvation (see John 16:8; Acts 7:51).

partakers of the Holy Spirit (v. 4)—See the notes on 2:4. Even though the concept of partaking is used in 3:1, 14; and 12:8 of a relationship which believers have, the context must be the final determining factor. This context in verses 4–6 seems to preclude a reference to true believers. It could be a reference to their participation, as noted above, in the miraculous ministry of Jesus who was empowered by the Spirit (see Luke 4:14, 18) or in the convicting ministry of the Holy Spirit (John 16:8), which obviously can be resisted without experiencing salvation.

tasted (v. 5)—See the note on verse 4. This has an amazing correspondence to what was described in 2:1–4. Like Simon Magus (Acts 8:9–24), these Hebrews had not yet been regenerated in spite of all they had heard and seen (see Matt. 13:3–9; John 6:60–66). They were repeating the sins of those who died in the wilderness after seeing the miracles performed through Moses and Aaron and hearing the voice of God at Sinai.

fall away (v. 6)—This Greek term occurs only here in the New Testament. In the LXX, it was used to translate terms for severe unfaithfulness and apostasy (see Ezek. 14:13; 18:24; 20:27). It is equivalent to the apostasy of 3:12. The seriousness of this unfaithfulness is seen in the severe description of rejection within this verse: they re-crucify Christ and treat Him contemptuously (see also the strong descriptions in 10:29). The "impossible" of verse 4 goes with "to renew them again to repentance." Those who sinned against Christ in such a way had no hope of restoration or forgiveness (see 2:2, 3; 10:26, 27; 12:25). The reason is that they had rejected Him with full knowledge and conscious experience (as described in the features of vv. 5, 6). With full revelation they rejected the truth, concluding the opposite of the truth about Christ, and thus had no hope of being saved. They can never have more knowledge than they had when they rejected it. They have concluded that Jesus should have been crucified, and they stand with his enemies. There is no possibility of these verses referring to losing salvation. Many Scripture passages make unmistakably clear that salvation is eternal. Those who want to make this verse mean that believers can lose salvation will have to admit that it would then also say that one could never get it back again.

rejected (v. 8)—See the use of the term in Romans 1:28 ("debased"); 2 Corinthians 13:5 ("disqualified"); and 2 Timothy 3:8 ("disapproved").

beloved (v. 9)—This term shows a change of audience and a change from a message of warning to a message of encouragement. That the address is to believers is further confirmed by the expression of confidence that "better things" could be said of them (as compared to those who were being warned in the preceding verses). The "things that accompany salvation" are their works which verify their salvation (v. 10; see Eph. 2:10; James 2:18, 26). The very statement implies that the things described in 5:11–6:5 do not accompany salvation but are indicative of unbelief and apostasy.

though we speak in this manner (v. 9)—Though it had been necessary to speak about judgment in the preceding verses, the writer assures the "beloved," those who are believers, that he is confident of their salvation.

toward His name (v. 10)—Throughout this epistle "name" has the Hebraic sense of the authority, character, and attributes of the Son of God (1:4) or of God the Father (2:12; 13:15; see John 14:13–14).

saints (v. 10)—All true Christians are saints, or "holy ones" (see 13:24; Acts 9:13; Rom. 1:7).

you (v. 11)—The author is speaking again to unbelievers but appears to intentionally distance this particular group from the would—be apostates of verses 4–6, who are in danger of being impossible to restore.

diligence (v. 11)—This term can carry the idea of eagerness or haste. It is a plea for unbelieving Jews to come to Christ immediately. If these uncommitted Jews followed the example of the active faith of the saints (vv. 9–10, 12), they would obtain the salvation which gives "full assurance of hope until the end" (see 10:22; Col 2:2). Salvation should not be postponed.

sluggish (v. 12)—See the note on 5:11, where the same Greek word is translated "dull."

imitate (v. 12)—This concept is repeated in 13:7 and is inherent in the many illustrations of faith given in chapter 11.

inherit the promises (v. 12)—The inheritance and the promises of salvation are a theme of this epistle (see vv. 13, 15, 17; 1:14; 4:1, 3; 9:15; 10:36; 11:7–9, 11, 13, 17, 33, 39).

Abraham (v. 13)—To encourage the Hebrews to rely upon faith as opposed to holding on to the Levitical system of worship, the writer cited the example of Abraham, who, as the great model of faith (see Rom. 4), should be imitated (v. 12).

swore by Himself (v. 13)—God promised unilaterally to fulfill the Abrahamic Covenant.

patiently endured (v. 15)—Abraham was an example of the patience mentioned in verse 12. He received the promise in the beginning of its fulfillment by the birth of Isaac (see the note on v. 14), but he did not live to see all the promises fulfilled (11:13).

two immutable things (v. 18)—These are God's promise and His oath. The Greek term behind "immutable" was used of a legal will, which was unchangeable by anyone but the maker of the will.

fled for refuge (v. 18)—In the LXX, the Greek word is used for the cities of refuge God provided for those who sought protection from avengers for an accidental killing (Num. 35:9–34; Josh. 20:1–9; see Acts 14:5–6).

hope (v. 18)—See the note on 3:6. Hope is one of the themes of Hebrews. It is also the product of Old Testament studies (Rom. 15:4). Hope for the fulfillment of God's salvation promises is the "anchor of the soul" (v. 19) keeping the believer secure during times of trouble and turmoil.

Understanding the Text

4) What does it mean that some of the recipients of the epistle are dull of hearing? What are the symptoms of this condition?

_____

_____

(verses to consider: Rom. 1:18–32)

5) How specifically does Hebrews contrast spiritually immature Jews with mature followers of Christ (vv. 12–14)?

_____

_____

6) Is Hebrews 6:1–8 a warning about losing one's salvation or a warning to those Jews who had heard the gospel and seen its power close-up but had never made a faith commitment to Christ? How do you know? How do the practices mentioned in this section shed light on this question?

_____

_____

(verses to consider: Ex. 30:18–21; Lev. 1:4; 3:8, 13; Acts 4:12; Titus 3:5)

7) What phrases are used to describe the Jews' experience of God's self-revelation? How much of God can a person experience and still not believe?

_____

_____

(verses to consider: Matt. 12:22–32; John 6; Acts 7:51; 8:9–24)

8) In 6:9 the author shifts from warning unbelievers to encouraging believers. What are the "better things" that "accompany salvation" that mark the difference between the "beloved" believers and the unbelievers of 5:11–6:8?

_____

_____

9) How does this passage encourage believers through the example of Abraham and the promises of God?

_____

_____

_____

Cross-Reference

Read Romans 8:35–39.

35 *Who shall separate us from the love of Christ? Shall tribulation, or distress, or persecution, or famine, or nakedness, or peril, or sword?*
36 *As it is written:*
"For Your sake we are killed all day long;
We are accounted as sheep for the slaughter."
37 *Yet in all these things we are more than conquerors through Him who loved us.*
38 *For I am persuaded that neither death nor life, nor angels nor principalities nor powers, nor things present nor things to come,*
39 *nor height nor depth, nor any other created thing, shall be able to separate us from the love of God which is in Christ Jesus our Lord.*

Exploring the Meaning

10) What does this passage say about true believers losing their salvation?

_____

_____

(verses to consider: John 10:27–29; Phil. 1:6; 1 Pet. 1:3–5)

11) Read Galatians 3:23–24. How does this passage add to your understanding of the "immature" or elementary nature of the Old Covenant?

_____

_____

12) Read 1 Thessalonians 1:2–4. How is the "labor of love" demonstrated by believers related to their salvation?

_____

_____

13) Read Titus 1:2. What does this passage say about the trustworthiness of God and the security of His promises—to both Jews and Gentiles?

_____

_____

Summing Up . . .

"The Christian life boils down to one thing: the measure of our love for the Lord. How preoccupied are we with His name—not with saying it sentimentally in a 'spiritual' tone or with vainly repeating it in our conversation and prayer—but with doing His will for the sake of His glory? How lofty and exalted is our view of God and how overwhelming are our concerns in genuine love for Him? When we love Him with all our 'heart and soul and mind and strength,' we will then be able—and only then be able—to love our neighbor as ourselves."—John MacArthur, _Hebrews_, Moody Press, 1983, p. 156.

Reflecting on the Text

14) What evidence in your life is there that Christ dwells in you and that you possess eternal life?

_____

_____

15) The passage studied in this lesson commends the believers' service and love in ministering to the saints. What concrete acts of service and demonstrations of love is God prompting you to engage in this week to someone in your faith community?

_____

_____

16) What specific promise of God do you need to cling to this week?

_____

_____

Recording Your Thoughts

_____

_____

_____

_____

_____

For further study, see the following passages:

Gen. 22:15–19	Deuteronomy 19:1–13	Romans 2:17–23; 3:1–2
1 Corinthians 2:14	Philippians 3:9	Colossians 3:16
1 Thessalonians 1:3–4	2 Timothy 3:15	Titus 3:5
1 Peter 3:15; 4:11		

Christ and Melchizedek

Opening Thought

1) What does your name mean? What name in the Bible do you find most intriguing? most humorous? most strange?

_____

_____

_____

_____

2) How does our society determine "greatness"? In what ways does this practice run contrary to God's standards?

_____

_____

_____

_____

3) What is something in your life or home that needs replacing? What is something you hope you never will have to get rid of? Why?

_____

_____

_____

_____

_____

Background of the Passage

Chapter 7 is clearly the focal point of Hebrews. It concerns the central, most significant, part of Judaism—the priesthood. Without the priests, no sacrifice could be made, and without the sacrifices no forgiveness of sins could be had. Obedience to the law was exceedingly important, but the offering of sacrifice was even more essential. And only the priesthood could offer them. It is no wonder that the priesthood was exalted in Judaism.

The writer first introduced Melchizedek (see Gen. 14) in chapter 5. There is much conjecture about the identity and nature of this mysterious Old Testament person. Nevertheless, it is best to view Melchizedek as an actual, historical human being, whose priestly ministry typifies that of Christ. In other words, Melchizedek was an ancient man whom God intended to serve as a picture of Jesus Christ. His life and ministry served as a frail illustration, very limited analogy to what Christ would later do during His earthly ministry.

In the same way that Melchizedek's priesthood was superior to the Levitical-Aaronic priesthood, so also was Christ's. Jesus' priesthood is universal, royal, righteous, peaceful, personal, and eternal. Christ's perfect and complete ministry far surpassed and superseded the old, imperfect, temporary system of sacrifices. This is the stunning message of chapter 7.

Bible Passage

Read 7:1–28, noting the key words and definitions to the right of the passage.

Hebrews 7:1–28

¹ *For this Melchizedek, king of Salem, priest of the Most High God, who met Abraham returning from the slaughter of the kings and blessed him,*

² *to whom also Abraham gave a tenth part of all, first being translated "king of righteousness," and then also king of Salem, meaning "king of peace,"*

³ *without father, without mother, without genealogy, having neither beginning of days nor end of life, but made like the Son of God, remains a priest continually.*

Melchizedek (v. 1)—a summary of the account of Melchizedek in Genesis 14:18–20

without father . . . (v. 3)—The Levitical priesthood was hereditary, but Melchizedek's was not. His parentage and origin are unknown because they were irrelevant to his priesthood. Contrary to some interpretations, Melchizedek did have a father and a mother. The ancient Syriac Peshitta gives a more accurate translation of what was intended by the Greek phrase: "whose

⁴ *Now consider how great this man was, to whom even the patriarch Abraham gave a tenth of the spoils.*

⁵ *And indeed those who are of the sons of Levi, who receive the priesthood, have a commandment to receive tithes from the people according to the law, that is, from their brethren, though they have come from the loins of Abraham;*

⁶ *but he whose genealogy is not derived from them received tithes from Abraham and blessed him who had the promises.*

⁷ *Now beyond all contradiction the lesser is blessed by the better.*

⁸ *Here mortal men receive tithes, but there he receives them, of whom it is witnessed that he lives.*

⁹ *Even Levi, who receives tithes, paid tithes through Abraham, so to speak,*

¹⁰ *for he was still in the loins of his father when Melchizedek met him.*

¹¹ *Therefore, if perfection were through the Levitical priesthood (for under it the people received the law), what further need was there that another priest should rise according to the order of Melchizedek, and not be called according to the order of Aaron?*

¹² *For the priesthood being changed, of necessity there is also a change of the law.*

¹³ *For He of whom these things are spoken belongs to another tribe, from which no man has officiated at the altar.*

¹⁴ *For it is evident that our Lord arose from Judah, of which tribe Moses spoke nothing concerning priesthood.*

¹⁵ *And it is yet far more evident if, in the likeness of Melchizedek, there arises another priest*

¹⁶ *who has come, not according to the law of a fleshly commandment, but according to the power of an endless life.*

¹⁷ *For He testifies:*

father and mother are not written in genealogies." No record existed of Melchizedek's birth or death. This is quite a contrast to the details of Aaron's death.

like (v. 3)—This means literally "made to be like"; this word is used nowhere else in the New Testament. The implication is that the resemblance to Christ rests upon the way Melchizedek's history is reported in the Old Testament, not upon Melchizedek himself. Melchizedek was not the pre-incarnate Christ, as some maintain, but was similar to Christ in that his priesthood was universal (v. 1), royal (v. 1–2; see Zech. 6:13), righteous (v. 2; see Ps. 72:2; Jer. 23:5; 1 Cor. 1:30), peaceful (v. 2; see Ps. 72:7; Is. 9:6; Rom. 5:1), and unending (v. 3; see v. 24–25).

Abraham gave a tenth (v. 4)—In antiquity, it was common for people to give a tithe to a god or his representative. Abraham, the father of the Hebrew faith, gave a tithe to Melchizedek. That proves that Melchizedek was superior to Abraham. The lesser person tithes to the greater (v. 7).

to receive tithes (v. 5)—By the authority invested in them after the establishment of the Mosaic law, the Levitical priests collected tithes from their fellow Israelites. The submission of the Israelites was not to honor the priests but to honor the law of God.

the lesser is blessed by the better (vv. 6–7)—Melchizedek not only received a tithe from Abraham but also he blessed him. This proves again Melchizedek's superiority.

Here . . . there (v. 8)—The adverbs have reference to the Levitical law whose system was still active at the time ("here") and to the earlier historical incident recorded in Genesis 14 ("there"). The Levitical priesthood changed

*"You are a priest forever
According to the order of Melchizedek."*

18 *For on the one hand there is an annulling of the former commandment because of its weakness and unprofitableness,*

19 *for the law made nothing perfect; on the other hand, there is the bringing in of a better hope, through which we draw near to God.*

20 *And inasmuch as He was not made priest without an oath*

21 *(for they have become priests without an oath, but He with an oath by Him who said to Him:
"The LORD has sworn
And will not relent,
'You are a priest forever
According to the order of Melchizedek' "),*

22 *by so much more Jesus has become a surety of a better covenant.*

23 *Also there were many priests, because they were prevented by death from continuing.*

24 *But He, because He continues forever, has an unchangeable priesthood.*

25 *Therefore He is also able to save to the uttermost those who come to God through Him, since He always lives to make intercession for them.*

26 *For such a High priest was fitting for us, who is holy, harmless, undefiled, separate from sinners, and has become high er than the heavens;*

27 *who does not need daily, as those high priests, to offer up sacrifices, first for His own sins and then for the people's, for this He did once for all when He offered up Himself.*

28 *For the law appoints as high priests men who have weakness, but the word of the oath, which came after the law, appoints the Son who has been perfected forever.*

as each priest died until it passed away altogether, whereas Melchizedek's priesthood is perpetual since the record about his priesthood does not record his death (see v. 3).

Levi . . . paid tithes (vv. 9–10)—In an argument based upon seminal headship, the writer observes that it is possible to speak of Levi paying tithes to Melchizedek. It is the same kind of argument Paul employed to demonstrate that when Adam sinned we all sinned.

perfection (v. 11)—See the note on 5:14. Throughout Hebrews, the term refers to complete reconciliation with and access to God—salvation. The Levitical system and its priesthood could not save anyone from their sins. See the notes on 10:1–4.

a change of the law (vv. 12–14)—since Christ is the Christian's high priest and He was of the tribe of Judah, not Levi (see Rev. 5:5), His priesthood is clearly beyond the law which was the authority for the Levitical priesthood (see v. 11). This is proof that the Mosaic law had been abrogated. The Levitical system was replaced by a new Priest, offering a new sacrifice, under a New Covenant. He abrogated the law by fulfilling it (see Matt. 5:17) and providing the perfection which the law could never accomplish (see Matt. 5:20).

another (vv. 13, 15)—In both cases, the term is "another of a different kind" emphasizing the contrast with the Levitical priesthood.

fleshly commandment (v. 16)—The law dealt only with the temporal existence of Israel. The forgiveness which could be obtained even on the Day of Atonement was temporary. Those who ministered as priests under the law were mortals receiving their office by heredity. The Levitical system was dominated by matters of physical existence and transitory ceremonialism.

power of an endless life (v. 16)—Because He is the eternal Second Person of the Godhead, Christ's priesthood cannot end. He obtained His priesthood, not by virtue of the law, but by virtue of His deity.

annulling (v. 18)—See the note on verses 12–14. The law was weak in that it could not save or bring about inward change in a person.

the law made nothing perfect (v. 19)—See the note on verse 11. The law saved no one; rather it cursed everyone.

a better hope (v. 19)—See the notes on 3:6; 6:18.

draw near to God (v. 19)—See Introduction: Historical and Theological Themes; see the note on 4:16. This is the key phrase in this passage. Drawing near to God is the essence of Christianity as compared with the Levitical system, which kept people outside His presence. As believer priests, we are all to draw near to God—that is a characteristic of priesthood.

oath (vv. 20–21)—God's promises are unchangeable, sealed with an oath (see 6:17). The Melchizedekan priesthood of Christ is confirmed with God's oath in Psalm 110:4. God's mind on this matter will not change ("relent," v. 21).

surety (v. 22)—This is the only use of the Greek term in the New Testament and could also be translated "guarantor." Jesus Himself guarantees the success of His New Covenant of salvation.

a better covenant (v. 22)—The New Covenant (8:8, 13; 9:15). See Matthew 26:28. The first mention of "covenant" in this epistle is coupled with one of the key themes of the book ("better," see v. 19; see Introduction: Historical and Theological Themes). This covenant will be more fully discussed in chapter 8.

many. (v. 23)—It is claimed that there were eighty-four high priests served from Aaron until the destruction of the temple by the Romans in A.D. 70. The lesser priests' numbers were much larger.

uttermost (v. 25)—virtually the same concept as was expressed in "perfection" (v. 11) and "make perfect" (v. 19)

who come to God (v. 25)—See the note on 4:16.

intercession (v. 25)—The word means "to intercede on behalf of another." It was used to refer to bringing a petition to a king on behalf of someone. Since rabbis assigned intercessory powers to angels, perhaps the people were treating angels as intercessors. The writer makes it clear that only Christ is the intercessor.

Holy . . . undefiled, separate from sinners (v. 26)—In His relationship to God, Christ is "holy" (without any pollution; Matt. 17:5; Acts 13:35). In His relationship to man, He is "harmless" (without evil or malice; John 8:46). In relationship to Himself, He is "undefiled" (free from contamination) and "separate from sinners" (He had no sin nature to be the source of any act of sin; see "without sin" in 4:15).

daily (v. 27)—Whenever the Levitical high priest sinned, he was required to offer sacrifices for himself (Lev. 4:3). Whenever the people sinned, he also had to offer a sacrifice for them (Lev. 4:13). These occasions could be daily. Then, annually, on the Day of Atonement, he had to again offer sacrifices for himself and for the people (Lev. 16:6, 11, 15). Christ had no sin and needed no sacrifice for Himself. And only one sacrifice (by Him) was needed—one time only, for all men, for all time.

once for all (v. 27)—key emphasis in Hebrews. The sacrificial work of Christ never needed to be repeated, unlike the Old Testament priestly sacrifices. See 9:12, 26, 28; 10:2, 10; 1 Peter 3:18.

word of the oath (v. 28)—God confirmed Christ as high priest. See the notes on verses 20–21; 6:16–18.

Understanding the Text

4) Who was Melchizedek, what does his name mean, and what was his connection to Abraham?

_____

_____

_____

(verses to consider: Gen. 14:17–20; Ps. 110:4; Heb. 5:6–10; 6:20)

5) How did Melchizedek's life and ministry typify the later life and ministry of Jesus Christ?

_____

_____

_____

6) How is Jesus unique among those who served as priests before God? In what ways does chapter 7 portray his priesthood as superior to that of the Old Covenant?

_____

_____

_____

Cross-Reference

Read Numbers 8:5–25.

⁵ Then the LORD spoke to Moses, saying:

⁶ "Take the Levites from among the children of Israel and cleanse them ceremonially.

⁷ "Thus you shall do to them to cleanse them: Sprinkle water of purification on them, and let them shave all their body, and let them wash their clothes, and so make themselves clean.

⁸ *"Then let them take a young bull with its grain offering of fine flour mixed with oil, and you shall take another young bull as a sin offering.*

⁹ *"And you shall bring the Levites before the tabernacle of meeting, and you shall gather together the whole congregation of the children of Israel.*

¹⁰ *"So you shall bring the Levites before the Lᴏʀᴅ, and the children of Israel shall lay their hands on the Levites;*

¹¹ *"and Aaron shall offer the Levites before the Lᴏʀᴅ, like a wave offering from the children of Israel, that they may perform the work of the Lᴏʀᴅ.*

¹² *"Then the Levites shall lay their hands on the heads of the young bulls, and you shall offer one as a sin offering and the other as a burnt offering to the Lᴏʀᴅ, to make atonement for the Levites.*

¹³ *"And you shall stand the Levites before Aaron and his sons, and then offer them like a wave offering to the Lᴏʀᴅ.*

¹⁴ *"Thus you shall separate the Levites from among the children of Israel, and the Levites shall be Mine.*

¹⁵ *"After that the Levites shall go in to service the tabernacle of meeting. So you shall cleanse them and offer them, like a wave offering.*

¹⁶ *"For they are wholly given to Me from among the children of Israel; I have taken them for Myself instead of all who open the womb, the firstborn of all the children of Israel.*

¹⁷ *"For all the firstborn among the children of Israel are Mine, both man and beast; on the day that I struck all the firstborn in the land of Egypt I sanctified them to Myself.*

¹⁸ *"I have taken the Levites instead of all the firstborn of the children of Israel.*

¹⁹ *"And I have given the Levites as a gift to Aaron and his sons from among the children of Israel, to do the work for the children of Israel in the tabernacle of meeting, and to make atonement for the children of Israel, that there be no plague among the children of Israel when the children of Israel come near the sanctuary."*

²⁰ *Thus Moses and Aaron and all the congregation of the children of Israel did to the Levites; according to all that the Lᴏʀᴅ commanded Moses concerning the Levites, so the children of Israel did to them.*

²¹ *And the Levites purified themselves and washed their clothes; then Aaron presented them, like a wave offering before the Lᴏʀᴅ, and Aaron made atonement for them to cleanse them.*

²² *After that the Levites went in to do their work in the tabernacle of meeting before Aaron and his sons; as the Lᴏʀᴅ commanded Moses concerning the Levites, so they did to them.*

²³ *Then the Lᴏʀᴅ spoke to Moses, saying,*

²⁴ *"This is what pertains to the Levites: From twenty-five years old and above one*

may enter to perform service in the work of the tabernacle of meeting;
25 *"and at the age of fifty years they must cease performing this work, and shall work no more."*

7) What does the passage say about the Levitical priesthood? What were the limitations of this Old Testament priesthood?

_____

_____

_____

Exploring the Meaning

8) Read Matthew 27:50–51. What is the significance of verse 51 and how does it relate to Christ's priesthood?

_____

_____

_____

9) Read Jeremiah 31:31–34. How is the arrangement brought about by Christ a "better covenant?"

_____

_____

_____

10) Read Romans 8:34. What does it mean that Christ intercedes for us?

_____

_____

_____

(verses to consider: John 17; 1 Tim. 2:5)

Summing Up . . .

"Jesus was undefiled, free from any moral or spiritual blemish. Think about it. For thirty-three years Jesus Christ was in the world, mingling continually with sinners and being tempted continually by Satan. Yet He never contracted the least taint of sin or defilement. Just as the rays of the sun can shine into the foulest stagnant pond and not lose their radiance and purity, so Jesus lived his life in the sinful, defiled world without losing the least of His beauty and purity. He moved through the world and remained untouched by any of its blemishes. He came into the most direct and personal contact with Satan, yet left as spotless as before they met. There never was a priest who was undefiled—until Jesus."—John MacArthur, *Hebrews*, Moody Press, 1983, p. 202.

Reflecting on the Text

11) What does it mean for you personally that Jesus Christ is our High Priest forever?

_____

_____

_____

12) How can the truths revealed in this chapter and lesson give you more confidence to draw near to God in any and every circumstance?

_____

_____

_____

13) What changes need to take place in your prayer life as a result of this study?

_____

_____

_____

Recording Your Thoughts

_____

_____

_____

_____

_____

_____

_____

_____

_____

_____

_____

_____

_____

_____

_____

_____

_____

_____

_____

_____

_____

_____

For further study, see the following passages:

Exodus 19:22	Numbers 20:22–29	Matthew 2:1, 6; 3:17
Mark 1:24	Luke 4:24	John 6:37; 8:46
Acts 2:27	Romans 3:19, 20	Romans 5:12–14; 8:3
2 Corinthians 5:21	Galatians 3:10–13; 4:9	1 Peter 1:19

A Better Covenant

Opening Thought

1) What is the best:

_____ restaurant in your town?

_____ brand of vehicle one can buy?

_____ holiday of the year?

_____ way to spend a free day?

_____ book you've ever read?

_____ Bible story?

2) What is the best "deal" you've ever found? What made this transaction such a bargain?

_____

3) Does "new" always equal "improved"? Why or why not?

_____

4) Are you the kind of person who hangs on to old possessions (for example, cars, appliances, computers, etc.) as long as possible before replacing them? Or do you like to trade-in and trade-up on a regular basis? Why?

_____

_____

Background of the Passage

The New Covenant is the primary focus in chapter 8. The High priest of this New Covenant is, of course, Jesus Christ, who occupies a unique seat at the right hand of God the Father (v. 1). Christ's sanctuary or place of ministry under this new arrangement is not an earthly tabernacle, but a heavenly one (vv. 2–5). There He continues to minister on behalf of His people—bringing their heartfelt gifts (i.e., their worship, praise, repentance, dedication, thanksgiving, etc.) to the Father (vv. 6–13).

Jesus' superior seat and His superior sanctuary are clear evidences of His superior ministry. His superior ministry is evidence of the superior nature of the New Covenant, which He mediates and which has superior promises. The Old Covenant was an impersonal, external legal code written on tablets of stone and given to a nation that merely provided for the temporary covering of sin. The New Covenant, on the other hand, promised an internal law written on the hearts of individuals. It provided full and final forgiveness of sin. And, more important, it also provided a new power for individuals to live as they ought.

In short, this chapter poses and answers two questions: (1) "Why should a Jew be satisfied with the old priesthood and the old sacrifices—which are only copies and shadows of forgiveness and reconciliation—when he can have real forgiveness and real reconciliation in Jesus Christ?" And (2) "What Old Covenant priest could compare with Jesus Christ, the incomparable High priest of the New Covenant?"

Bible Passage

Read 8:1–13, noting the key words and definitions to the right of the passage.

Hebrews 8:1–13

¹ Now this is the main point of the things we are saying: We have such a High priest, who is seated at the right hand of the throne of the Majesty in the heavens,

² a Minister of the sanctuary and of the true tabernacle which the Lord erected, and not man.

³ For every high priest is appointed to offer both

High priest . . . seated at the right hand of the throne of the Majesty in the heavens (vv. 1–5)—A brief description of Jesus' priesthood in the heavenly sanctuary, which is better than Aaron's because He serves in a better sanctuary (vv. 1–5; see 9:1–12)

main point (v. 1)—Here the writer arrived at his central message. The fact is that "we have" (current pos-

gifts and sacrifices. Therefore it is necessary that this One also have something to offer.

⁴ For if He were on earth, He would not be a priest, since there are priests who offer the gifts according to the law;

⁵ who serve the copy and shadow of the heavenly things, as Moses was divinely instructed when he was about to make the tabernacle. For He said, "See that you make all things according to the pattern shown you on the mountain."

⁶ But now He has obtained a more excellent ministry, inasmuch as He is also Mediator of a better covenant, which was established on better promises.

⁷ For if that first covenant had been faultless, then no place would have been sought for a second.

⁸ Because finding fault with them, He says: "Behold, the days are coming, says the LORD, when I will make a new covenant with the house of Israel and with the house of Judah—

⁹ "not according to the covenant that I made with their fathers in the day when I took them by the hand to lead them out of the land of Egypt; because they did not continue in My covenant, and I disregarded them, says the LORD.

¹⁰ "For this is the covenant that I will make with the house of Israel after those days, says the LORD: I will put My laws in their mind and write them on their hearts; and I will be their God, and they shall be My people.

¹¹ "None of them shall teach his neighbor, and none his brother, saying, 'Know the LORD,' for all shall know Me, from the least of them to the greatest of them.

¹² "For I will be merciful to their unrighteousness, and their sins and their lawless deeds I will remember no more."

¹³ In that He says, "A new covenant," He has made the first obsolete. Now what is becoming obsolete and growing old is ready to vanish away.

session) a superior high priest, Jesus Christ, who is the fulfillment of all that was foreshadowed in the Old Testament.

seated (v. 1)—See the notes on 1:3, 13.

Minister (v. 2)—This is the same word used of the angels in 1:7. In Jeremiah 33:21 it was used of the priests.

sanctuary (v. 2)—see 9:3; the holiest place where God dwelt (see Ex. 26:23, 24)

true tabernacle (v. 2)—The definition is given in the phrase "which the Lord erected, and not man," as well as in 9:11, 24 (see v. 5). It refers to the heavenly dwelling place of God.

gifts and sacrifices (v. 3)—See the note on 5:1.

not be a priest (v. 4)—Jesus was not qualified to be a Levitical priest because He was not of the tribe of Levi. See the note on 7:12–14. Because of its use of the present tense, this verse indicates that the Levitical system was still in operation at the time of writing, indicating it was before the destruction of the temple in A.D. 70 (see the note on 5:1–4).

"For He said . . . "(v. 5)—The quote is from Exodus 25:40.

copy and shadow (v. 5)—This does not mean that there are actual buildings in heaven which were copied in the tabernacle, but rather that the heavenly realities were adequately symbolized and represented in the earthly tabernacle model.

Mediator (v. 6)—See 9:15. The word describes a go-between or an arbitrator, in this case between man and God.

better covenant . . . better promises (v. 6)—See the notes on 7:19, 22. This covenant is identified as the "new covenant" in verses 8, 13; 9:15.

if that first covenant had been faultless (v. 7)—See the same argument in 7:11. The older covenant, incomplete and imperfect, was only intended to be temporary.

I disregarded them (v. 9)—Jeremiah 31:32 says, "though I was a husband to them." The New Testament writer is quoting from the LXX, which uses a variant reading that does not essentially change the meaning.

mind . . . hearts (v. 10)—By its nature, the Covenant of Law was primarily external, but the New Covenant is internal (see Ezek. 36:26, 27).

ready to vanish (v. 13)—Soon after the Book of Hebrews was written, the temple in Jerusalem was destroyed and its Levitical worship ended (See the note on 5:1–4; see Introduction: Author and Date).

Understanding the Text

5) Where is Christ right now? What is significant about the statement that He "is seated"?

_____

_____

(verses to consider: Heb. 10:11; Rev. 3:21)

6) How do earthly temples and tabernacles contrast with the heavenly sanctuary in which Christ is now serving?

_____

_____

7) How does this chapter demonstrate the superiority of the New Covenant over the Old Covenant? Give specifics.

_____

_____

Cross-Reference

Read Jeremiah 31:31–34.

³¹ *"Behold, the days are coming, says the LORD, when I will make a new covenant with the house of Israel and with the house of Judah—*
³² *"not according to the covenant that I made with their fathers in the day that I*

took them by the hand to lead them out of the land of Egypt, My covenant which they broke, though I was a husband to them, says the LORD.

³³ "But this is the covenant that I will make with the house of Israel after those days, says the LORD: I will put My law in their minds, and write it on their hearts; and I will be their God, and they shall be My people.

³⁴ "No more shall every man teach his neighbor, and every man his brother, saying, 'Know the LORD,' for they all shall know Me, from the least of them to the greatest of them, says the LORD. For I will forgive their iniquity, and their sin I will remember no more."

8) How do you think the original hearers of this revelation of a coming New Covenant must have reacted to such news?

_____

_____

Exploring the Meaning

9) Read Ezekiel 36:26–27. How does the New Covenant affect internal heart change?

_____

_____

(verses to consider: Ezek. 11:19–20; John 14:17; 2 Corinthians 3:6)

10) Read Colossians 1:21 and 1 Timothy 2:5. What is the job of a mediator? Why is it necessary to have a mediator between God and man? Why is Christ the only one who can truly fill that role?

_____

_____

Summing Up . . .

"The Old Covenant symbol is not bad, and never was bad. It had a beautiful, God-given purpose. It pointed to the Son, represented the Son, foreshadowed the Son before He came to earth. But now that the Son has come, the symbol has no more purpose, and God means for it to be discarded. . . .

"The old sacrificial system actually was over when the veil was split in two and Christ's sacrifice was complete (Matt. 27:50–51; Mark 15:37–39; Luke 23:44–46). At that time, Christ's unique, never-to-be-repeated sacrifice was finished with the result that all men in Christ had direct access to God (1 Tim. 2:3–6). The destruction of the Temple completed the closing of the Old Covenant—by removing the place of sacrifice that no longer served a purpose. The age of the Mosaic law and the Levitical priests was over. The age of the Son was come forever."—John MacArthur, *Hebrews*, Moody Press, 1983, p. 217.

Reflecting on the Text

11) How do you think you might view sin differently if you were still required to bring animal sacrifices to a priest on an ongoing basis ?

_____

_____

12) How could you use the good news of God's New Covenant to help someone who is trying to earn God's favor?

_____

_____

13) What are some specific and practical ways you can show your gratitude to Christ for the fact that He has dealt finally and decisively with your sins?

_____

_____

Recording Your Thoughts

For further study, see the following passages:

Exodus 15:17; 25:8   1 Chronicles 22:17   John 1:17
Galatians 3:19–20   1 Timothy 2:5

A Better Sanctuary

Hebrews 9:1–14

Opening Thought

1) What two objects could you use to help tell the story of your spiritual journey? Why are these items significant?

_____

_____

_____

2) What is something in your life (a habit, hobby, possession, dream, etc.) that would be extremely difficult for you to give up? Why?

_____

_____

3) What is the most beautiful or unusual religious shrine, cathedral, or church that you've ever visited? What made it so memorable?

_____

_____

4) Give some examples where the old "version" of an item is superior to the new. How about where the new "model" is an improvement over the old?

_____

_____

Background of the Passage

God never asks anyone to give up anything without His offering something far better in exchange. The chief obstacle in the way of the Hebrews' faith was their failure to see that everything connected with the ceremonial law (covenant, sacrifices, priesthood, and ritual) was preparatory and transient. So the writer painstakingly and definitively pursues a clear explanation of the better character of the New Covenant.

This is the subject of Hebrews 9:1–14—the further contrast of the Old and New Covenants. The first part of the passage (vv. 1–10) outlines, or summarizes, the characteristics of the Old (its sanctuary, services, and significance), whereas the second part (vv.11–14) high lights the characteristics of the New (its sanctuary, services, and significance).

The point of this passage was not to demean the old way of relating to God, but rather to show its shadowy incompleteness. To condense and paraphrase verses 13 and 14, God is saying, "If the old things were so good as mere symbols, how much better are the final realities they symbolize. If the external, physical, and temporary covenant accomplished its purpose so well, how much better will the internal, spiritual, and eternal covenant accomplish its purpose?"

Bible Passage

Read 9:1–14, noting the key words and definitions to the right of the passage.

Hebrews 9:1–14

¹ *Then indeed, even the first covenant had ordinances of divine service and the earthly sanctuary.*

² *For a tabernacle was prepared: the first part, in which was the lampstand, the table, and the showbread, which is called the sanctuary;*

³ *and behind the second veil, the part of the tabernacle which is called the Holiest of All,*

⁴ *which had the golden censer and the ark of the covenant overlaid on all sides with gold, in which were the golden pot that had the manna, Aaron's*

a tabernacle (vv. 1–10)—In these verses, the author gives a brief description of the tabernacle, to which some fifty chapters in the Old Testament are devoted, including the tabernacle service (see Ex. 25–40). The section is marked off by its beginning with a reference to "ordinances" (v. 1) and closing with a reference to "ordinances" (v. 10).

first part . . . sanctuary (v. 2) —This is the Holy Place, the first room of the tabernacle. For the items in the Holy Place, see Exodus 40:22–25.

Holiest of All (v. 3)—This is the Most Holy Place where the ark of

rod that budded, and the tablets of the covenant;

5 *and above it were the cherubim of glory overshadowing the mercy seat. Of these things we cannot now speak in detail.*

6 *Now when these things had been thus prepared, the priests always went into the first part of the tabernacle, performing the services.*

7 *But into the second part the high priest went alone once a year, not without blood, which he offered for himself and for the people's sins committed in ignorance;*

8 *the Holy Spirit indicating this, that the way into the Holiest of All was not yet made manifest while the first tabernacle was still standing.*

9 *It was symbolic for the present time in which both gifts and sacrifices are offered which cannot make him who performed the service perfect in regard to the conscience—*

10 *concerned only with foods and drinks, various washings, and fleshly ordinances imposed until the time of reformation.*

11 *But Christ came as High priest of the good things to come, with the greater and more perfect tabernacle not made with hands, that is, not of this creation.*

12 *Not with the blood of goats and calves, but with His own blood He entered the Most Holy Place once for all, having obtained eternal redemption.*

13 *For if the blood of bulls and goats and the ashes of a heifer, sprinkling the unclean, sanctifies for the purifying of the flesh,*

14 *how much more shall the blood of Christ, who through the eternal Spirit offered Himself without spot to God, cleanse your conscience from dead works to serve the living God?*

the covenant and the mercy seat dwelt—the place of atonement (Ex. 26:33–34).

golden censer (v. 4)—This is best understood as being the golden altar of incense (see Ex. 40:5, 26–27). Though it was outside the Most Holy Place (Ex. 30:6), the writer of Hebrews pictures the golden altar inside the Most Holy Place because uppermost in his mind is its role in the liturgy of the Day of Atonement. On that day, the high priest brought incense from that altar into the Most Holy Place. The altar of golden incense marked the boundary of the Most Holy Place as well as the curtain. The high priest went beyond the altar of incense only once a year.

the ark (v. 4)—See Exodus 25:10–18.

golden pot that had the manna (v. 4)—See Exodus 16:32–36.

Aaron's rod (v. 4)—See Numbers 17:2–10.

tablets of the covenant (v. 4) —See Exodus 25:16 (see 1Kin. 8:9).

cherubim . . . mercy seat (v. 5)—See Exodus 25:17–18.

cannot now speak in detail (v. 5)—The writer has no desire to obscure his main point with details (see 8:1).

once a year (v. 7)—This was the Day of Atonement.

not without blood (v. 7)—See the note on verse 22. This is the first of many references to the blood of sacrifice. The term is especially central to 9:1–10:18 where it identifies the deaths of Old Testament sacrifices and of Christ (see vv.12–14). Note, however, that the shedding of blood in and of itself is an insufficient sacrifice. Christ had not only to shed His blood, but to die. Hebrews 10:10 indicates that He gave His body as the sacrificial offering. Without His death, His blood had no saving value.

the way . . . was not yet made manifest (v. 8)—The Levitical system did not provide any direct access into God's presence for His people. Rather, it kept them away. Nearness had to be provided by another way (v. 12). This is the primary lesson which the Holy Spirit taught concerning the tabernacle. It teaches how inaccessible God is apart from the death of Jesus Christ. See Introduction: Historical and Theological Themes. See the counterpart to this lesson in 10:20.

Holy Spirit (v. 8)—See the note on 2:4. By the Spirit-inspired instruction given for the Holiest of All, He was indicating that there was no way to God in the ceremonial system. Only Christ could open the way.

symbolic (v. 9)—The Greek word is parabole from which the English word "parable" is derived. The Levitical system was a parable, an object lesson, about what was to come in Christ.

for the present time (v. 9)—"For" is ambiguous enough to allow for two different meanings and interpretations: (1) "during" the time of the Old Testament, or (2) "until" and "pointing to" the current Christian era. The NKJV's translation "in which" indicates the first interpretation. The second interpretation is "according to which" (from an alternate Greek reading) referring to the "parable" rather than to the time, "It was an object lesson from the past pointing to the present time." This latter interpretation is preferable because of the explanation in verse 10. "The present time" is "the time of reformation."

perfect . . . conscience (v. 9)—Again, this term refers to salvation. The sacrifices of the Old Testament did not remove the offerers' guilty consciences or provide them with full forgiveness for their sins (see 10:1–4). It was only "symbolic" of something else that would—namely Christ. The conscience is a divinely given warning device that reacts to sin and produces accusation and guilt (see the notes on Rom. 2:14–15) that cannot be relieved apart from the work of Christ (see v. 14; 10:22). At the time of salvation it is quieted from its convicting ravings, but it is not deactivated. Rather, it continues its work, warning the believer about sin. Believers should seek a clear conscience (see 2 Corinthians 1:12).

foods and drinks (v. 10)—See Deuteronomy 14:3–21.

fleshly ordinances (v. 10)—The Levitical ordinances regulated the visible actions without changing the inner man (see 10:4).

reformation (v. 10)—The Greek term means "restoring what is out of line." All things are set straight in Christ. The reformation is the New Covenant and its application. (See the note on v. 9.)

the good things to come (v. 11)—The reference appears to be to the "eternal redemption" (v. 12). In 10:1, the "good things" refer back to the "salvation" of verse 28. Most Greek editions of the New Testament accept the reading "that have come." In the context, both readings refer to the things of the New Covenant. It is just a matter of perspective: whether from the viewpoint of the Levitical system where the realities of redemption were "to come," or the viewpoint of those in the Christian era where the realities of redemption "have come" because Christ has completed His work.

not of this creation (v. 11)—The phrase is the explanation of "not made with hands"—it is the creation of God alone. The sanctuary where Christ serves is heaven itself (see v. 24; 8:2).

goats and calves (v. 12)—Only one of each was sacrificed on the Day of Atonement (see Lev. 16:5–10). The plural here represents the numbers sacrificed as the Day of Atonement was observed year after year.

with His own blood (v. 12)—A better translation would be "through His own blood." The same phrase is used in 13:12. Nothing is said to indicate that Christ carried His actual physical blood with Him into the heavenly sanctuary. The Sacrificer was also the Sacrifice.

once for all (v. 12)—See the note on 7:27.

eternal redemption (v. 12)—This word for redemption is found only here and in Luke 1:68; 2:38. Its original use was for the release of slaves by payment of a ransom.

ashes of a heifer (v. 13)—It is said that, in the history of Israel, only six red heifers were killed and their ashes used. One heifer's ashes would suffice for centuries since only a minute amount of the ash was required.

unclean (v. 13)—The Greek term is literally "common" or "profane." Not that it was ceremonially unclean, but it was not sanctified or set apart unto God. The word was used in Jesus' discourse on what defiles a man (see Matt. 15:11, 18, 20; Mark 7:15, 18, 20, 23), in the Jews' complaint that Paul had defiled the temple by bringing Gentiles into it (Acts 21:28), and in reference to the meats that Peter had been invited to eat (Acts 10:15; 11:9). According to the Mosaic regulation, the red heifer's ashes were to be placed "outside the camp" and used in a ceremony for symbolic purifying from sin (Num. 19:9; see 13:11–13).

how much more (v. 14)—Superior to the cleansing capability of the ashes of an animal is the cleansing power of the sacrifice of Christ.

the blood of Christ (v. 14)—This is an expression that refers not simply to literal blood, but to the whole atoning sacrificial work of Christ in His death. Blood is used as a substitute word for death.

the eternal Spirit (v. 14)—See the note on 2:4. Some interpreters argue that the lack of the definite article in the Greek makes this a reference to Christ's own "eternal spirit" (in the sense of an endless life, see 7:16). However, the references to the Holy Spirit in 2:4 and 6:4 are also without the definite article. The use of "eternal" as a qualifier serves to relate the Spirit to the "eternal redemption" (v. 12) and the "eternal inheritance" (v. 15) which Christ accomplished by His sacrificial death.

offered Himself (v. 14)—See the notes on verse 7. The animals in the Levitical system were brought involuntarily and without understanding to their deaths. Christ came of His own volition with a full understanding of the necessity and consequences of His sacrifice. His sacrifice was not just His blood, it was His entire human nature (see 10:10).

without spot (v. 14)—In the LXX, the term is used for describing acceptable sacrifices including the red heifer (Num. 19:3; see Ex. 29:1; Lev. 1:3).

conscience (v. 14)—See the note on verse 9.

dead works (v. 14)—Their works are dead because the unregenerate are "dead in trespasses and sins," their works are worthless and unproductive (Gal. 5:19–21), and they end in death.

to serve the living God (v. 14)—Salvation is not an end in itself. The believer has been freed from sin to serve God, saved to serve (see Rom. 6:16–18; 1 Thess. 1:9). The contrast between dead works and the living God (see 3:12; 10:31; 12:22) is basic. (See James 2:14–26.)

Understanding the Text

5) How are the Old and New Covenants contrasted in this passage?

	Old	New
Sanctuary	_____	_____
Services	_____	_____
Significance	_____	_____

6) Why is the blood of Christ so significant?

_____

_____

_____

(verses to consider: Matt. 26:27–28; Rom. 3:23–26; 5:8, 9; Eph. 1:7; Col. 1:13, 14, 19–20)

7) How was Christ's sacrifice for sin different from the normal sacrifices for sin (v. 14)?

_____

_____

_____

(verses to consider: John 10:17–18; 1 Pet. 1:18–21)

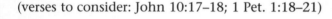

Cross-Reference

Read Leviticus 16:1–34.

¹ *Now the Lord spoke to Moses after the death of the two sons of Aaron, when they offered profane fire before the Lord, and died;*
² *and the Lord said to Moses: "Tell Aaron your brother not to come at just any time into the Holy Place inside the veil, before the mercy seat which is on the ark, lest he die; for I will appear in the cloud above the mercy seat.*
³ *"Thus Aaron shall come into the Holy Place: with the blood of a young bull as a sin offering, and of a ram as a burnt offering.*
⁴ *"He shall put the holy linen tunic and the linen trousers on his body; he shall be girded with a linen sash, and with the linen turban he shall be attired. These are holy garments. Therefore he shall wash his body in water, and put them on.*
⁵ *"And he shall take from the congregation of the children of Israel two kids of the goats as a sin offering, and one ram as a burnt offering.*
⁶ *"Aaron shall offer the bull as a sin offering, which is for himself, and make atonement for himself and for his house.*
⁷ *"He shall take the two goats and present them before the Lord at the door of the tabernacle of meeting.*

⁸ *"Then Aaron shall cast lots for the two goats: one lot for the LORD and the other lot for the scapegoat.*

⁹ *"And Aaron shall bring the goat on which the LORD's lot fell, and offer it as a sin offering.*

¹⁰ *"But the goat on which the lot fell to be the scapegoat shall be presented alive before the LORD, to make atonement upon it, and to let it go as the scapegoat into the wilderness.*

¹¹ *"And Aaron shall bring the bull of the sin offering, which is for himself, and make atonement for himself and for his house, and shall kill the bull as the sin offering which is for himself.*

¹² *"Then he shall take a censer full of burning coals of fire from the altar before the LORD, with his hands full of sweet incense beaten fine, and bring it inside the veil.*

¹³ *"And he shall put the incense on the fire before the LORD, that the cloud of incense may cover the mercy seat that is on the Testimony, lest he die.*

¹⁴ *"He shall take some of the blood of the bull and sprinkle it with his finger on the mercy seat on the east side; and before the mercy seat he shall sprinkle some of the blood with his finger seven times.*

¹⁵ *"Then he shall kill the goat of the sin offering, which is for the people, bring its blood inside the veil, do with that blood as he did with the blood of the bull, and sprinkle it on the mercy seat and before the mercy seat.*

¹⁶ *"So he shall make atonement for the Holy Place, because of the uncleanness of the children of Israel, and because of their transgressions, for all their sins; and so he shall do for the tabernacle of meeting which remains among them in the midst of their uncleanness.*

¹⁷ *"There shall be no man in the tabernacle of meeting when he goes in to make atonement in the Holy Place, until he comes out, that he may make atonement for himself, for his household, and for all the assembly of Israel.*

¹⁸ *"And he shall go out to the altar that is before the LORD, and make atonement for it, and shall take some of the blood of the bull and some of the blood of the goat, and put it on the horns of the altar all around.*

¹⁹ *"Then he shall sprinkle some of the blood on it with his finger seven times, cleanse it, and consecrate it from the uncleanness of the children of Israel.*

²⁰ *"And when he has made an end of atoning for the Holy Place, the tabernacle of meeting, and the altar, he shall bring the live goat.*

²¹ *"Aaron shall lay both his hands on the head of the live goat, confess over it all the iniquities of the children of Israel, and all their transgressions, concerning all their sins, putting them on the head of the goat, and shall send it away into the wilderness by the hand of a suitable man.*

²² *"The goat shall bear on itself all their iniquities to an uninhabited land; and he shall release the goat in the wilderness.*

23 *"Then Aaron shall come into the tabernacle of meeting, shall take off the linen garments which he put on when he went into the Holy Place, and shall leave them there.*

24 *"And he shall wash his body with water in a holy place, put on his garments, come out and offer his burnt offering and the burnt offering of the people, and make atonement for himself and for the people.*

25 *"The fat of the sin offering he shall burn on the altar.*

26 *"And he who released the goat as the scapegoat shall wash his clothes and bathe his body in water, and afterward he may come into the camp.*

27 *"The bull for the sin offering and the goat for the sin offering, whose blood was brought in to make atonement in the Holy Place, shall be carried outside the camp. And they shall burn in the fire their skins, their flesh, and their offal.*

28 *"Then he who burns them shall wash his clothes and bathe his body in water, and afterward he may come into the camp.*

29 *"This shall be a statute forever for you: In the seventh month, on the tenth day of the month, you shall afflict your souls, and do no work at all, whether a native of your own country or a stranger who dwells among you.*

30 *"For on that day the priest shall make atonement for you, to cleanse you, that you may be clean from all your sins before the LORD.*

31 *"It is a sabbath of solemn rest for you, and you shall afflict your souls. It is a statute forever.*

32 *"And the priest, who is anointed and consecrated to minister as priest in his father's place, shall make atonement, and put on the linen clothes, the holy garments;*

33 *"then he shall make atonement for the Holy Sanctuary, and he shall make atonement for the tabernacle of meeting and for the altar, and he shall make atonement for the priests and for all the people of the assembly.*

34 *"This shall be an everlasting statute for you, to make atonement for the children of Israel, for all their sins, once a year."* And he did as the LORD commanded Moses.

8) What features of the solemn Day of Atonement make the biggest impression on you? Why?

_____

_____

_____

_____

Exploring the Meaning

9) Read Ephesians 2:4–6. What does it mean (and why does it matter) that spiritually speaking we are already with Christ in the heavenly places?

_____

_____

_____

(verses to consider: Acts 7:48–50; 17:24; Phil. 3:20)

10) Read 2 Corinthians 5:17. How does Christ's appropriated sacrifice differ from the efficacy of the Old Testament sacrifices? In other words, what kind of lasting change did Christ's death on the cross make possible?

_____

_____

_____

Summing Up . . .

"If the Old Covenant, weak and imperfect as it was, served its purpose, how much better will Christ's New Covenant, powerful and perfect, serve its purpose. The new not only has a better purpose, but accomplishes its purpose in a better way, a perfect way. The purpose of the old sacrifice was to symbolize, externally, the cleansing of sin. It accomplished this purpose. The purpose of the new sacrifice, however, was to cleanse actually, internally (where sin really exists). It accomplished its purpose in a superior way. . . .

"The former priests cleaned up the outside, and even that only symbolically, imperfectly, and temporarily. But Christ cleanses from the inside, where the real problem is. He does more than cleanse the old man; He replaces it with a new man. He cleanses our conscience, but He recreates our person. In Christ, we are not cleaned-up old creatures but redeemed new creatures (2 Corinthians 5:17)."—John MacArthur, *Hebrews*, Moody Press, 1983, p. 230.

Reflecting on the Text

11) What is the solution for a Christian who struggles with a guilty conscience? What specific truths or principles should you recall the next time you approach God in prayer or worship?

_____

_____

12) What Old Testament religious custom or ritual do you understand more completely as a result of this study? What practice do you wish to understand even more clearly? How will you go about this?

_____

_____

13) The sacrifice that Christ made in becoming a man and dying on the cross—in offering Himself willingly for this—ought to inspire us with a deep sense of gratitude. In what ways can your heart and life reflect a greater sense of thankfulness for the superior sacrifice of Christ? Spend some time in prayer thanking God that Christ's death made it possible to "receive the promise of the eternal inheritance."

_____

_____

Recording Your Thoughts

_____

_____

For further study, see the following passages:

Exodus 16:32–36	Exodus 25:23–40	Exodus 26:32–36
Leviticus 11:1–47; 24:5–9	Numbers 17:2–10	Isaiah 42:1; 61:1
Matthew 26:28	Luke 4:1, 14	John 14:6
Acts 20:26	Romans 5:9; 6:23; 10:15	Galatians 2:16
Ephesians 2:1	Colossians 2:16	

A Better Sacrifice

Opening Thought

1) How old were you when death first become a reality to you? What happened?

_____

_____

_____

_____

2) What are some of the more common ways that people face (or refuse to face!) their own mortality?

_____

_____

_____

_____

3) How much would you be willing to pay for the following items if it meant you'd never have to buy them again?

• Blue jeans? _____

• A vehicle? _____

• A television? _____

•A lawnmower? _____

• Cosmetics/personal care items? _____

Background of the Passage

Some Christians question how Old Testament believers were saved, since salvation is only through Jesus Christ (Acts 4:12), and the details of Christ's life, death, and resurrection were not known in their lifetime. The answer is that Old Testament saints were saved on the same basis as believers today are saved—by the finished work of Christ. The point being made here (9:15) is that Christ's atoning death was retroactive. So the Old Testament sacrifices were not means of salvation, but marks of faithful obedience and hopeful symbols of the one perfect sacrifice that would be the means of salvation.

This subject, the death of Christ, had long been a stumbling block to the Jews. A dying Messiah contradicted their deeply held theological presuppositions. Being very much aware of this theological blind spot, the writer of Hebrews proceeded to give three reasons it was necessary for Messiah to die: a testament demands death (9:16–17), forgiveness demands blood (9:18–26), and judgment demands a substitute (9:27–28).

While chapter 9 demonstrates the absolute necessity of Messiah's sacrifice, 10:1–18 reveals the character of His sacrifice. Christ crucified is the only hope of men. That is the idea. Here is a record of Jesus' death from the theological, rather than the historical, standpoint. We are reminded of the ineffectiveness of the old sacrifices. We are shown the meaning and the depth of His death in all of its richness. In His death, Jesus was the perfect sacrifice for sin.

Bible Passage

Read 9:15–10:18, noting the key words and definitions to the right of the passage.

Hebrews 9:15—10:18

15 *And for this reason He is the Mediator of the new covenant, by means of death, for the redemption of the transgressions under the first covenant, that those who are called may receive the promise of the eternal inheritance.*

16 *For where there is a testament, there must also of necessity be the death of the testator.*

death (v. 15)—In the making of some biblical covenants, sacrifices were involved. When God made the covenant with Abraham, five different animals were sacrificed in the ceremony (Gen. 15:9–10). The Mosaic Covenant was affirmed by animal sacrifices (Ex. 24:5–8).

redemption (v. 15)—The compound term used here is found more frequently than the term used in verse 12 (see 11:35; Luke 21:28).

17 For a testament is in force after men are dead, since it has no power at all while the testator lives.

18 Therefore not even the first covenant was dedicated without blood.

19 For when Moses had spoken every precept to all the people according to the law, he took the blood of calves and goats, with water, scarlet wool, and hyssop, and sprinkled both the book itself and all the people,

20 saying, "This is the blood of the covenant which God has commanded you."

21 Then likewise he sprinkled with blood both the tabernacle and all the vessels of the ministry.

22 And according to the law almost all things are purified with blood, and without shedding of blood there is no remission.

23 Therefore it was necessary that the copies of the things in the heavens should be purified with these, but the heavenly things themselves with better sacrifices than these.

24 For Christ has not entered the holy places made with hands, which are copies of the true, but into heaven itself, now to appear in the presence of God for us;

25 not that He should offer Himself often, as the high priest enters the Most Holy Place every year with blood of another—

26 He then would have had to suffer often since the foundation of the world; but now, once at the end of the ages, He has appeared to put away sin by the sacrifice of Himself.

27 And as it is appointed for men to die once, but after this the judgment,

28 so Christ was offered once to bear the sins of many. To those who eagerly wait for Him He will appear a second time, apart from sin, for salvation.

10:1 For the law, having a shadow of the good things

Jesus' death retroactively redeemed all those who had believed in God under the Old Covenant (see Rom. 3:24–26). This is in keeping with the symbolism of the Day of Atonement. Annually the high priest would atone for or cover the sins that the people had committed in the preceding year (Lev. 16:16, 21, 30).

first covenant (v. 15)—The actual first covenant historically was made with Noah (Gen. 6:18; 9:9). Next came the covenant made with Abraham (Gen. 15:18). By context, however, the older covenant under discussion in this epistle is that which is called the Mosaic Covenant or the Covenant of Law (Ex. 19: 1–20:21). "First" in this verse, therefore, means the former, older covenant with which the Levitical system is connected.

those who are called (v. 15)—Literally "the ones having been called," this phrase looks back to those under the Old Covenant who were called to salvation by God on the basis of the sacrifice of Jesus Christ to come long after most of them had died. The reference, as always in the New Testament epistles, is to the effectual calling related to salvation (see 3:1), which in this context refers to Old Testament believers.

promise of the eternal inheritance (v. 15)—that is, salvation in its fullness (see the notes on "rest" in 3:11; 4:1, 9; 6:12)

testament (v. 16)—A last will and testament illustrates the necessity of Christ's death. "Testament" is the same Greek word translated "covenant," but the term takes on the more specialized meaning in this context. The benefits and provisions of a will are only promises until the one who wrote the will dies. Death activates the promises into realities.

blood (v. 18)—"Death" in verses 15–16 is replaced by "blood" (see the notes on vv. 7, 14). The term is used to emphasize the violent aspect of His sacrificial death.

water, scarlet wool, and hyssop (v. 19)—These items were

to come, and not the very image of the things, can never with these same sacrifices, which they offer continually year by year, make those who approach perfect.

2 For then would they not have ceased to be offered? For the worshipers, once purified, would have had no more consciousness of sins.

3 But in those sacrifices there is a reminder of sins every year.

4 For it is not possible that the blood of bulls and goats could take away sins.

5 Therefore, when He came into the world, He said:
"Sacrifice and offering You did not desire,
But a body You have prepared for Me.

6 In burnt offerings and sacrifices for sin
You had no pleasure.

7 Then I said, 'Behold, I have come—
In the volume of the book it is written of Me—
To do Your will, O God.' "

8 Previously saying, "Sacrifice and offering, burnt offerings, and offerings for sin You did not desire, nor had pleasure in them" (which are offered according to the law),

9 then He said, "Behold, I have come to do Your will, O God." He takes away the first that He may establish the second.

10 By that will we have been sanctified through the offering of the body of Jesus Christ once for all.

11 And every priest stands ministering daily and offering repeatedly the same sacrifices, which can never take away sins.

12 But this Man, after He had offered one sacrifice for sins forever, sat down at the right hand of God,

13 from that time waiting till His enemies are made His footstool.

14 For by one offering He has perfected forever those who are being sanctified.

15 But the Holy Spirit also witnesses to us; for after He had said before,

used at the Passover in Egypt for sprinkling of blood, and in the ritual cleansing for lepers, and in the red heifer ceremony (Num. 19:6). More of those are in view here. These elements were a part of the sprinkling of blood in the covenant ceremony described in Exodus 24:1–8, though not mentioned there. The added details came either by direct revelation to the writer or had been preserved in other records or traditions known to the writer and his readers.

the book . . . the people (v. 19)—See the notes on Exodus 24:1–8. The consecration of Aaron and his sons to the priesthood is the only other occasion in the Old Testament when any persons were sprinkled with blood. The detail about the book also being sprinkled with the blood is not recorded in the Exodus account.

This is the blood (v. 20)—The same formula was utilized in the inaugural ceremonies for the Mosaic Covenant and for the New Covenant.

likewise (v. 21)—The dedication of the tabernacle and its vessels was accompanied by a blood-sprinkling ritual similar to that observed at the inauguration of the Mosaic Covenant (see Ex. 29:10–15, 21, 36, 37).

almost all (v. 22)—There were a few exceptions. Water, incense, and fire were also used to purify (see Ex. 19:10; Lev. 15:5; Num. 16:46, 47; 31:21–24). Those who were too poor to bring even a small animal for sacrifice were allowed to bring fine flour instead.

blood . . . remission (v. 22) —"It is the blood that makes atonement for the soul." The phraseology is reminiscent of Christ's own words. "Shedding of blood" refers to death (see the notes on vv. 7, 14, 18). "Remission" (meaning forgiveness) is the emphatic last word in this section (vv. 18–22) of the Greek New Testament, and it forms the transition to the next section (vv. 23–28).

copies (v. 23)—The earthly tabernacle and its vessels were only

16 *"This is the covenant that I will make with them after those days, says the LORD: I will put My laws into their hearts, and in their minds I will write them,"*

17 *then He adds, "Their sins and their lawless deeds I will remember no more."*

18 *Now where there is remission of these, there is no longer an offering for sin.*

symbolic replicas of the true heavenly tabernacle (8:2) and were also made unclean by the transgressions of the people (Lev. 16:16).

the heavenly things (v. 23)—As the preceding context indicated, the inauguration of the Mosaic Covenant by sacrifices was necessary (vv. 18–21). That concept is here applied to the heavenly sanctuary—it is dedicated or inaugurated as the central sanctuary of the New Covenant by Christ's sacrifice. The better covenant required a better sacrifice.

better sacrifices (v. 23)—Christ's superior sacrifice is a major theme in 9:13–10:18. The many sacrifices of the Levitical system were to be superseded by better sacrifices that would be represented in the one, all-inclusive, perfect sacrifice of Christ (see 10:12).

copies (v. 24)—The term is not the same as that used in v. 23 and 8:5. This is literally "antitype." It is used only twice in the New Testament. The antitype either prefigures the type (as here), or is a later illustration of the type. In both cases, the antitype is not the real thing, but only a copy of it. The earthly "holy places" in the tabernacle were only types of the heavenly abode of God.

now to appear (v. 24)—On the Day of Atonement, the high priest entered the Most Holy Place where God made an appearance (Lev. 16:2). The high priest, however, was hidden from the presence of God by the cloud of incense (Lev. 16:12, 13). (See also "has appeared" (v. 26) and "will appear" (v. 28).) Each verb is a different term in the Greek. The term for Christ's present appearance in heaven (v. 24) alludes to His official presentation to report to the Father on the fulfillment of His mission. The concept of making an appearance or being revealed is involved in the incarnational appearance in order to die once for sin (v. 26). At Christ's appearing at the Second Advent (v. 28), the term used stresses the visible nature of the appearance (see 2:8; 12:14). All three tenses of Christ's soteriological ministry are also covered: (1) His First Advent to save us from the penalty of sin; (2) His present intercessory ministry in heaven to save us from the power of sin; and (3) His Second Advent to deliver us from the presence of sin.

for us (v. 24)—Christ is our representative and the provider of our spiritual benefits (see 2:9; 6:20; 7:25; John 14:12–14).

since the foundation of the world (v. 26)—This is a reference to creation.

end of the ages (v. 26)—All the eras and ages came together and were consummated in the coming of the Messiah. The eschatological era was inaugurated (see the note on 1:2).

to die once (v. 27)—This is a general rule for all humankind. There have been very rare exceptions; for example, Lazarus died twice. Those, like Lazarus, who were raised from the dead by a miraculous act of our Lord were not resurrected to a glorified body and unending life. They only experienced resuscitation. Another exception will be those who don't die (for example, Enoch, Elijah) even once, but who will be "caught up . . . to meet the Lord in the air."

the judgment (v. 27)—a general term encompassing the judgment of all people, believers and unbelievers

second time (v. 28)—On the Day of Atonement, the people eagerly waited for the high priest to come back out of the Most Holy Place. When he appeared, they knew that the sacrifice on their behalf had been accepted by God. In the same way, when Christ appears at His second coming, it will be confirmation that the Father has been fully satisfied with the Son's sacrifice on behalf of believers. At that point salvation will be consummated.

apart from sin (v. 28)—See the notes on 2:17–18; 4:15. This phrase testifies to the completed work of Christ in removing sins by His sacrifice at His first coming. No such burden will be upon Him in His second coming.

shadow (v. 10:1)—The Greek term translated "shadow" refers to a pale reflection, as contrasted with a sharp, distinct one. The term behind "very image," on the other hand, indicates an exact and distinct replica (see Col. 2:17).

perfect (v. 1)—This term is used repeatedly in Hebrews to refer to salvation. See 5:14; 7:11; 9:9. As much as those living under the law desired to approach God, the Levitical system provided no way to enter His holy presence (see Ps. 15:1; 16:11; 24:3–4).

consciousness of sins (v. 2)—This is the same word translated "conscience" in verse 10:22; 9:9; 13:18. See the note on 9:9. If sin had really been overpowered by that system of sacrifices, the Old Testament believers' consciences would have been cleansed from condemning guilt (see v. 22). There was not freedom of conscience under the Old Covenant.

reminder (v. 3)—The Old Testament sacrifices not only could not remove sin, but their regular repetition was a regular reminder of that deficiency. The promise of the New Covenant was that the sin would be removed and even God would "remember" their sins "no more" (8:12, quoting Jer. 31:34).

not possible (v. 4)—The Levitical system was not designed by God to remove or forgive sins. It was preparatory for the coming of the Messiah in that it made the people expectant. It revealed the seriousness of their sinful condition, in that even temporary covering required the death of an animal. It revealed the reality of God's holiness and righteousness by indicating that sin had to be covered. Finally, it revealed the necessity of full and complete forgiveness so that God could have desired fellowship with His people.

You did not desire (vv. 5–6)—God was not pleased with sacrifices given by a person who did not give them out of a sincere heart (see Ps. 51:17; Is. 1:11; Jer. 6:20; Hos. 6:6; Amos 5:21–25). To sacrifice only as a ritual, without obedience, was a mockery and worse than no sacrifice at all (see Is. 1:11–18).

a body You have prepared for Me (v. 5)—Psalm 40:6 reads, "My ears you have opened." This does not represent a significant alteration in the meaning of the psalm. The writer is quoting the LXX translation of the Hebrew idiom. The Greek translators of the LXX regarded the Hebrew words as a figure of speech, in which a part of something signified the whole, i.e., the hollowing out of ears was part of the total work of fashioning a human body. And ears were selected as the part to emphasize because they were symbols of obedience as the organ of the reception of God's Word and will (see 1 Sam. 15:22). Christ needed a body in order to offer Himself as the final sacrifice (2:14).

to do Your will (v. 7)—See Matthew 26:39, 42.

first . . . second (v. 9)—The old, repetitious sacrificial system was removed to make way for the new, once-for-all sacrifice of Christ, who had obediently done God's will (see 5:8; Phil. 2:8).

sanctified (v. 10)— "Sanctify" means to "make holy," to be set apart from sin for God (see 1 Thess. 4:3). When Christ fulfilled the will of God, He provided for the believer a continuing, permanent condition of holiness (Eph. 4:24; 1 Thess. 3:13). This is the believer's positional sanctification, as opposed to the progressive sanctification that results from daily walking by the will of God.

body (v. 10)—This refers to His atoning death, as does the term blood (9:7, 12, 14, 18, 22). Mention of the body of Christ in such a statement is unusual in the New Testament, but it is logically derived from the quotation from Psalm 40:6.

stands (v. 11)—In 2 Chronicles 6:10, 12, Solomon sat on his throne as king, but stood at the altar when acting in a priestly role (see Deut. 17:12; 18:7).

footstool (v. 13)—This is yet another reference to Psalm 110:1. This prediction will be fulfilled when Christ returns and all creation acknowledges His lordship by bowing at His feet (Phil. 2:10).

perfected (v. 14)—This involves a perfect standing before God in the righteousness of Christ (see Rom. 3:22; Phil. 3:8–9).

Understanding the Text

4) What must happen in order for sins to be forgiven?

_____

_____

_____

(verses to consider: Matt. 26:27–28)

5) What does this passage teach about death? Who will evade death? What awaits men after death?

_____

_____

_____

(verses to consider: 2 Corinthians 5:10; 1 Thess. 4:17; Rev. 20:11–15)

6) In what ways was the Old Testament sacrificial system insufficient?

_____

Cross-Reference

Read Exodus 24:1–8.

¹ Now He said to Moses, "Come up to the Lord, you and Aaron, Nadab and Abihu, and seventy of the elders of Israel, and worship from afar.
² "And Moses alone shall come near the Lord, but they shall not come near; nor shall the people go up with him."
³ So Moses came and told the people all the words of the Lord and all the judgments. And all the people answered with one voice and said, "All the words which the Lord has said we will do."
⁴ And Moses wrote all the words of the Lord. And he rose early in the morning, and built an altar at the foot of the mountain, and twelve pillars according to the twelve tribes of Israel.
⁵ Then he sent young men of the children of Israel, who offered burnt offerings and sacrificed peace offerings of oxen to the Lord.
⁶ And Moses took half the blood and put it in basins, and half the blood he sprinkled on the altar.
⁷ Then he took the Book of the Covenant and read in the hearing of the people. And they said, "All that the Lord has said we will do, and be obedient."
⁸ And Moses took the blood, sprinkled it on the people, and said, "This is the blood of the covenant which the Lord has made with you according to all these words."

7) What is described in this passage and how does it relate to Hebrews 9–10?

_____

_____

_____

Exploring the Meaning

8) Read 1 Peter 1:16. How did the sacrifice of Christ serve to provide sanctification for believers?

_____

_____

_____

(verses to consider: 1 Thess. 4:3; 2 Pet. 1:3–4)

9) Read Psalm 2. How does this messianic psalm echo the truth communicated in Hebrews 10:13?

_____

_____

_____

Summing Up . . .

"In Communion, or the Lord's Supper, we remember Christ's sacrificial death, as He commanded us to do. But He is not re-sacrificed. The Lord commanded His disciples to remember His death, not to try to redo it. . . .

"The work of sacrifice is done. There will be no more. Forgiveness is already provided for those who trust in this one perfect sacrifice. Why would anyone want to go back to the old sacrifices, which were never finished and never effective? To reject is to have no other hope of forgiveness—ever.

"The Lord is not slow about His promise, as some count slowness, but is patient toward you, not wishing for any to perish but for all to come to repentance' (2 Pet. 3:9). Salvation—glorious and perfect salvation—is promised in the Old Covenant and purchased in the New."—John MacArthur, _Hebrews_, Moody Press, 1983, pp. 241, 257.

Reflecting on the Text

10) Who in your life needs to hear and understand the good news of Christ's once-for-all sacrifice for the sins of the world? How could you tactfully turn the conversation to spiritual things with this person or these persons?

_____
_____

11) Hebrews 10:7 records Messiah's supreme mission of carrying out the will of God the Father. In what areas do you need to have a more submissive and compliant spirit to the will of God?

_____

_____

_____

12) Write a short note or psalm of praise to Christ for His perfect sacrifice for sin that makes you completely accepted in the sight of God.

_____

_____

_____

Recording Your Thoughts

_____

_____

_____

_____

_____

_____

For further study, see the following passages:

Genesis 9:16; 15:9–10	Exodus 12:22; 24:5–8	Exodus 29:21
Leviticus 5:11; 8:30	Leviticus 14:4; 17:11	Psalm 40:6–9
Isaiah 53:12	Matthew 26:28	Romans 3:24–26
2 Corinthians 5:21	Galatians 4:4	Ephesians 1:3
Philippians 3:20	1 Peter 1:2–5; 2:24; 3:21	

All about Faith

Opening Thought

1) When in your life do you feel as though your faith was:
• strongest?

• simplest?

• shakiest?

What were the circumstances at each of those stages?

_____

_____

_____

2) Chapter 11 gives capsule summaries of the lives of many Old
Testament saints. How would an objective observer describe your
earthly life (if it were to end today)? What kind of epitaph, eulogy,
or summary would you like to have when your time on earth is
done?

_____

_____

_____

3) Who are your heroes in the faith and why?

_____

_____

_____

Background of the Passage

According to the Bible, there are only two ways to live. One way, by far the most common way, is to live by sight, to base your life on what you can see. This is the way of empiricism. The other way, far less common, is to live by faith, to base your life primarily and ultimately on what you cannot see. This is the Christian way.

Christians have never seen God, or Jesus Christ, or heaven, or hell, or Satan, or the Holy Spirit. We have never seen any of the people who wrote the Bible or an original book of the Bible. Though we see the results, we have never seen any of the actual virtues that God commands or any of the graces that He gives. Yet we are convinced of all these things by faith. We bank our earthly lives and our eternal destiny on things which we have never seen. That is the way the people of God have always lived. This is the life that pleases God.

The end of chapter 10 and all of chapter 11 comprise a comprehensive study of faith—what it is and what it looks like in a human life, as well as what fate awaits those who do not believe God's self-revelation.

Hebrews 10:19–25 speaks to the person who knows the truth of the gospel and makes a positive response to the claims of Christ. The next section (vv. 26–39) is by far the most serious and sobering warning of the five given in Hebrews. It deals with apostasy—the sin of renouncing the gospel.

Chapter 11, sometimes called "The Saints' Hall of Fame," "The Westminster Abbey of Scripture," and "The Faith Chapter," deals with the primacy and excellency of faith. Its forty verses form an honor roll of Old Testament saints who lived and died by faith.

The chapter makes clear that, from the time of Adam on, God has honored faith, not works. Works have always been commanded as a by-product of faith. They are never a—means of salvation. God does not tolerate or honor any self-imposed ethical system as a means of reaching him.

Bible Passage

Read 10:19–11:40, noting the key words and definitions to the right of the passage.

¹⁹ *Therefore, brethren, having boldness to enter the Holiest by the blood of Jesus,*

²⁰ *by a new and living way which He consecrated for us, through the veil, that is, His flesh,*

²¹ *and having a High priest over the house of God,*

²² *let us draw near with a true heart in full assurance of faith, having our hearts sprinkled from an evil conscience and our bodies washed with pure water.*

²³ *Let us hold fast the confession of our hope without wavering, for He who promised is faithful.*

²⁴ *And let us consider one another in order to stir up love and good works,*

²⁵ *not forsaking the assembling of ourselves together, as is the manner of some, but exhorting one another, and so much the more as you see the Day approaching.*

²⁶ *For if we sin willfully after we have received the knowledge of the truth, there no longer remains a sacrifice for sins,*

²⁷ *but a certain fearful expectation of judgment, and fiery indignation which will devour the adversaries.*

²⁸ *Anyone who has rejected Moses' law dies without mercy on the testimony of two or three witnesses.*

²⁹ *Of how much worse punishment, do you suppose, will he be thought worthy who has trampled the Son of God underfoot, counted the blood of the covenant by which he was sanctified a common thing, and insulted the Spirit of grace?*

³⁰ *For we know Him who said, "Vengeance is Mine, I will repay," says the Lord. And again, "The LORD will judge His people."*

³¹ *It is a fearful thing to fall into the hands of the living God.*

³² *But recall the former days in which, after you were illuminated, you endured a great struggle with sufferings:*

³³ *partly while you were made a spectacle both by*

---

brethren (v. 19)—See the note on 3:12. As on the earlier occasion, the writer addresses his Jewish brethren with an invitation to leave behind the Levitical system and to appropriate the benefits of the New Covenant in Christ.

boldness (v. 19)—or "confidence," an important emphasis in the epistle (see the note on 4:16); because of the high priestly ministry of Christ and His finished sacrifice, the Hebrews can enter boldly into the presence of God

new (v. 20)—In Greek, this word originally meant "newly slain," but was understood as "recent" when the epistle was written. The way is new because the covenant is new. It is not a way provided by the Levitical system.

living way (v. 20)—Though it is the path of eternal life, it was not opened by Christ's sinless life—it required His death. See the notes on 2:17–18; 4:16. The Hebrews were invited to embark on this way, which is characterized by the eternal life of the Son of God who loved them and gave Himself for them. The Christian faith was known as "the Way" among the Jews of Jerusalem as well as among the Gentiles (Acts 19:23). Those receiving this epistle understood quite clearly that the writer was inviting them to become Christians—to join those who had been persecuted for their faith. True believers in their midst were even then suffering persecution, and those who had not committed themselves to the Way were asked to become targets of the same persecution.

veil . . . flesh (v. 20)—When Jesus' flesh was torn at His crucifixion, so was the temple veil that symbolically separated men from God's presence (Matt. 27:51). When the high priest on the Day of Atonement entered the Most Holy Place, the people waited outside for him to return. When Christ entered the heavenly temple He did not

reproaches and tribulations, and partly while you became companions of those who were so treated;

34 for you had compassion on me in my chains, and joyfully accepted the plundering of your goods, knowing that you have a better and an enduring possession for yourselves in heaven.

35 Therefore do not cast away your confidence, which has great reward.

36 For you have need of endurance, so that after you have done the will of God, you may receive the promise:

37 "For yet a little while,
And He who is coming will come and will not tarry.

38 Now the just shall live by faith;
But if anyone draws back,
My soul has no pleasure in him."

39 But we are not of those who draw back to perdition, but of those who believe to the saving of the soul.

11:1 Now faith is the substance of things hoped for, the evidence of things not seen.

2 For by it the elders obtained a good testimony.

3 By faith we understand that the worlds were framed by the word of God, so that the things which are seen were not made of things which are visible.

4 By faith Abel offered to God a more excellent sacrifice than Cain, through which he obtained witness that he was righteous, God testifying of his gifts; and through it he being dead still speaks.

5 By faith Enoch was taken away so that he did not see death, "and was not found, because God had taken him"; for before he was taken he had this testimony, that he pleased God.

6 But without faith it is impossible to please Him, for he who comes to God must believe that He is, and that He is a rewarder of those who diligently seek Him.

return. Instead, He opened the curtain and exposed the Most Holy Place so that we could follow Him. Here "flesh" is used as was "body" (v. 10) and "blood" (9:7, 12, 14, 18, 22) to refer to the sacrificial death of the Lord Jesus.

let us draw near (v. 22)—Based on what had been written, this was the heart of the invitation to those in the assembly who had not come to Christ. The same invitation is found in the first New Testament book to be written, where James reveals the corollary of drawing near to God: God will draw near to you. Asaph taught that it is a good thing to draw near to God (Ps. 73:28). The full restoration of Israel to God's blessing is dependent upon their drawing near to Him (Jer. 30:18–22). In other words, it is an eschatological invitation coming to them in "these last days" (1:2). This verse describes the prerequisites for entering the presence of God: sincerity, security, salvation, and sanctification.

true heart (v. 22)—The Greek term behind "true" carries the ideas of being sincere, genuine, and without ulterior motive (see Jer. 24:7; Matt. 15:8). This one thing these particular Hebrews lacked: genuine commitment to Christ.

full assurance of faith (v. 22) —Utter confidence in the promises of God is intended by the phrase. Such confidence will result in heartfelt assurance or security, which will allow them to persevere through the coming trials. This is the first of a familiar triad: faith, hope (v. 23), and love (v. 24).

pure water (v. 22)—The imagery in this verse is taken from the sacrificial ceremonies of the Old Covenant, where blood was sprinkled as a sign of cleansing, and the priests were continually washing themselves and the sacred vessels in basins of clear water. The "washing with pure water" does not refer to Christian baptism, but to the Holy Spirit's purifying one's life by means of the Word of God. This is purely a

7 *By faith Noah, being divinely warned of things not yet seen, moved with godly fear, prepared an ark for the saving of his household, by which he condemned the world and became heir of the righteousness which is according to faith.*

8 *By faith Abraham obeyed when he was called to go out to the place which he would receive as an inheritance. And he went out, not knowing where he was going.*

9 *By faith he dwelt in the land of promise as in a foreign country, dwelling in tents with Isaac and Jacob, the heirs with him of the same promise;*

10 *for he waited for the city which has foundations, whose builder and maker is God.*

11 *By faith Sarah herself also received strength to conceive seed, and she bore a child when she was past the age, because she judged Him faithful who had promised.*

12 *Therefore from one man, and him as good as dead, were born as many as the stars of the sky in multitude—innumerable as the sand which is by the seashore.*

13 *These all died in faith, not having received the promises, but having seen them afar off were assured of them, embraced them and confessed that they were strangers and pilgrims on the earth.*

14 *For those who say such things declare plainly that they seek a homeland.*

15 *And truly if they had called to mind that country from which they had come out, they would have had opportunity to return.*

16 *But now they desire a better, that is, a heavenly country. Therefore God is not ashamed to be called their God, for He has prepared a city for them.*

17 *By faith Abraham, when he was tested, offered up Isaac, and he who had received the promises offered up his only begotten son,*

18 *of whom it was said, "In Isaac your seed shall be called,"*

New Covenant picture (Jer. 31:33; Ezek. 36:25–26).

hold fast (v. 23)—Holding on, or the perseverance of the saints, is the human side of eternal security. It is not something done to maintain salvation but is rather an evidence of salvation.

confession of our hope (v. 23) —affirmation of salvation

without wavering (v. 23)—The idea is not to follow any inclination that leads back to the Old Covenant. In other ancient literature, the same Greek term is used of enduring torture. Persecution will come (2 Tim. 3:12), but God is faithful. Temptations will abound, but God is faithful to provide an escape (see 1 Cor. 10:13). God's promises are reliable (1 Cor. 10:13; 1 Thess. 5:24; Jude 24–25). With that confidence, the believer can persevere.

consider (v. 24)—The same verb is used about Jesus in 3:1. The invitation must be responded to individually, but the response also has a corporate side. They are members of a community of Hebrews whose initial attraction to Christ is in danger of eroding. They have been considering a return to the Levitical system of Judaism to avoid the persecution (see John 12:42–43). Mutual encouragement to make full commitment is crucial.

stir up (v. 24)—The English word "paroxysm" is derived from the Greek term used here. The meaning in this context is that of stimulating or inciting someone to do something.

love and good works (v. 24)— An example of such mutual effort in the midst of persecution was to be found at Corinth.

not forsaking the assembling (v. 25)—Collective and corporate worship is a vital part of spiritual life. The warning here is against apostasy in an eschatological context (see 2 Thess. 2:1). The

¹⁹ *concluding that God was able to raise him up, even from the dead, from which he also received him in a figurative sense.*

²⁰ *By faith Isaac blessed Jacob and Esau concerning things to come.*

²¹ *By faith Jacob, when he was dying, blessed each of the sons of Joseph, and worshiped, leaning on the top of his staff.*

²² *By faith Joseph, when he was dying, made mention of the departure of the children of Israel, and gave instructions concerning his bones.*

²³ *By faith Moses, when he was born, was hidden three months by his parents, because they saw he was a beautiful child; and they were not afraid of the king's command.*

²⁴ *By faith Moses, when he became of age, refused to be called the son of Pharaoh's daughter,*

²⁵ *choosing rather to suffer affliction with the people of God than to enjoy the passing pleasures of sin,*

²⁶ *esteeming the reproach of Christ greater riches than the treasures in Egypt; for he looked to the reward.*

²⁷ *By faith he forsook Egypt, not fearing the wrath of the king; for he endured as seeing Him who is invisible.*

²⁸ *By faith he kept the Passover and the sprinkling of blood, lest he who destroyed the firstborn should touch them.*

²⁹ *By faith they passed through the Red Sea as by dry land, whereas the Egyptians, attempting to do so, were drowned.*

³⁰ *By faith the walls of Jericho fell down after they were encircled for seven days.*

³¹ *By faith the harlot Rahab did not perish with those who did not believe, when she had received the spies with peace.*

³² *And what more shall I say? For the time would fail me to tell of Gideon and Barak and Samson and Jephthah, also of David and Samuel and the prophets:*

reference is to the approaching "Day" (the second coming of Christ; see 1 Cor. 3:13).

exhorting (v. 25)—Exhortation takes the form of encouragement, comfort, warning, or strengthening. There is an eschatological urgency to the exhortation which requires an increased activity as the coming of Christ approaches (see 3:13).

we (v. 26)—The author is speaking rhetorically. In verse 39, he excludes himself and genuine believers from this category.

sin willfully (v. 26)—The Greek term carries the idea of deliberate intention that is habitual. The sin is rejecting Christ deliberately. These are not isolated acts. According to the Mosaic legislation, such acts of deliberate, premeditated sin required exclusion from the congregation of Israel (see Num. 15:30, 31) and from its worship (see Ex. 21:14). Such sins also excluded the individual from sanctuary in the cities of refuge (see Deut. 19:11–13).

knowledge (v. 26)—The Greek term denotes specific knowledge, not general spiritual knowledge (see 6:4; see 1 Tim. 2:4). Though the knowledge was not defective or incomplete, the application of the knowledge was certainly flawed. Judas Iscariot is a good example of a disciple who had no lack of knowledge but lacked faith and became the arch-apostate.

no longer (v. 26)—The apostate is beyond salvation because he has rejected the only sacrifice that can cleanse him from sin and bring him into God's presence. To turn away from that sacrifice leaves him with no saving alternative. This is parallel to Matthew 12:31.

fearful expectation (v. 27)— The judgment is certain to happen, so it engenders fear.

judgment and fiery indignation (v. 27)—Ultimately, such judg-

33 *who through faith subdued kingdoms, worked righteousness, obtained promises, stopped the mouths of lions,*

34 *quenched the violence of fire, escaped the edge of the sword, out of weakness were made strong, became valiant in battle, turned to flight the armies of the aliens.*

35 *Women received their dead raised to life again. And others were tortured, not accepting deliverance, that they might obtain a better resurrection.*

36 *Still others had trial of mockings and scourgings, yes, and of chains and imprisonment.*

37 *They were stoned, they were sawn in two, were tempted, were slain with the sword. They wandered about in sheepskins and goatskins, being destitute, afflicted, tormented—*

38 *of whom the world was not worthy. They wandered in deserts and mountains, in dens and caves of the earth.*

39 *And all these, having obtained a good testimony through faith, did not receive the promise,*

40 *God having provided something better for us, that they should not be made perfect apart from us.*

ment is that of eternity in the lake of fire (see Matt. 13:38–42, 49–50).

adversaries (v. 27)—actual opposition against God and toward the program of God in salvation

how much worse punishment (v. 29)—There will be degrees of punishment in hell. This is also clearly indicated in Matthew 11:22–24.

trampled (v. 29)—In the ancient Near East one of the gestures used to show contempt for someone was to "lift up the foot" against or toward them (see Ps. 41:9). To walk on top of someone or something was a more extreme gesture showing utter contempt and scorn (see 2 Kin. 9:33; Is. 14:19; Mic. 7:10; Zech. 10:5). Such contempt demonstrates a complete rejection of Christ as Savior and Lord.

counted . . . common (v. 29)—To reckon Christ's blood as something "common" is the same thing as saying that it is unclean or defiled (See the note on 9:13) and implies that Christ was a sinner and a blemished sacrifice. Such thinking is truly blasphemous.

blood of the covenant (v. 29) —See the notes on 9:14–15. Christ's death inaugurated or ratified the New Covenant.

sanctified (v. 29)—This refers to Christ, in that He was set apart unto God (see John 17:19). It cannot refer to the apostate, because only true believers are sanctified. See Introduction: Interpretive Challenges.

insulted the Spirit of grace (v. 29)—See the notes on 6:4 and 9:14. The same title is utilized in Zechariah 12:10. Rejecting Christ insults the Spirit who worked through Him (Matt. 12:31–32) and who testifies of Him (John 15:26; 16:8–11).

recall (v. 32)—Carries the idea of carefully thinking back and reconstructing something in one's mind, not merely remembering (see Acts 5:41; 2 Cor. 7:15).

a great struggle (v. 32)—The word is only here in the New Testament. It is a picture of the struggling athlete engaged in a rigorous contest. After being enlightened, they suffered (v. 33), became offended, and began to fall away (see Matt. 13:20–21).

a spectacle (v. 33)—The theater is alluded to with regard to the actors being placed on a stage where they can be observed by everyone. In the context of this verse, the idea is exposure to disgrace and ridicule.

companions (v. 33)—These unconverted Hebrews had been close to persecution when it happened to the believers they associated with. They perhaps had actually suffered for that identification, including the seizure of their property, but had not yet turned away because they were still interested in the prospects of heaven (v. 34). In the New Testament, there are examples of those who willingly exposed themselves to possible arrest and harassment because they sought to help those who were persecuted for their faith. Surprisingly, on one occasion, the Pharisees were among them. The Pharisees warned Jesus about Herod's pending attempt on His life (Luke 13:31). Among genuine believers who might be given as examples of helping the persecuted, there was Onesiphorus (2 Tim. 1:16–18).

in my chains (v. 34)—This is one of the supposed indicators used for identifying the author of this epistle as the apostle Paul (see Eph. 3:1; 2 Tim. 1:8). However, many other Christians were also imprisoned.

a better and an enduring possession (v. 34)—See the note on 9:15 (see Matt. 6:19–20; 1 Pet. 1:4).

cast away (v. 35)—Due to their current persecutions, they were tempted to run away from their outward identification with Christ and Christians and to apostatize (see v. 23; Deut. 32:15, 18).

reward (v. 35)—They are closer than ever to the eternal reward. It is no time to turn back.

done the will of God (v. 36)—To trust in Christ fully by living daily in the will of the Father. (See Matt. 7:21–27; James 1:22–25.)

receive the promise (v. 36)—See the notes on 4:1; 6:12; 9:15. If they would but remain with the New Covenant and put their trust exclusively in Christ, they would obtain the promise of salvation for themselves.

the just shall live by faith (v. 38)—The opposite of apostasy is faith. This is a preview of the subsequent chapter. It is faith which pleases God. The individual who draws back from the knowledge of the gospel and faith will be guilty of his apostasy.

substance (v. 11:1)—This is from the same Greek word translated "express image" in 1:3 and "confidence" in 3:14. The faith described here involves the most solid possible conviction, the God-given present assurance of a future reality.

evidence of things not seen (v. 1)—True faith is not based on empirical evidence but on divine assurance and is a gift of God.

elders (v. 2)—Meaning "men of old." In this context, the term refers to all saints, both men and women, under the older covenant, a select few of whom are described in verses 4–40.

obtained a good testimony (v. 2)—literally "were testified to" or "had witness given about them" (see vv. 4, 39); God bears witness on the behalf of these saints that they lived by faith and divine approval is granted to them

By faith (v. 3)—Each example of faith in verses 3–31 is formally introduced with this specific phrase. True saving faith works in obedience to God (see James 2:14–26).

we (v. 3)—This refers to the writer and all other true believers, present and past.

worlds (v. 3)—the physical universe itself, as well as its operation and administration

were framed (v. 3)—The concept involved in this verb (used also in 13:21) is that of equipping so that something might be made ready to fulfill its purpose.

word of God (v. 3)—God's divine utterance (see, for example, Gen. 1:3, 6, 9, 11, 14)

not made (v. 3)—God created the universe out of something which cannot be seen. There is the possibility that the invisible something was God's own energy or power.

more excellent (v. 4)—The precise reason for the excellence of Abel's sacrifice is not specifically revealed by the writer of Hebrews but implied in 12:24 (see the notes there). Here his concern is with Abel's faith. Both brothers knew what God required. Abel obeyed and Cain did not. Abel acted in faith, Cain in unbelief.

through which . . . it (v. 4)—The antecedent of both "which" and "it" is Abel's faith, not his offering. Through that faith, he left testimony to all succeeding generations that a person comes to God by faith to receive righteousness.

righteous (v. 4)—Because of his faith, evidenced in obedience to God's requirement for sacrifice, Abel was accounted as righteous by God (see Rom. 4:4–8). Christ Himself referred to the righteousness of Abel (Matt. 23:35). Cain's sacrifice was evidence that he was just going through the motions of ritual in a disobedient manner, not evidencing authentic faith. Without faith no one can receive imputed righteousness (see Gen. 15:6).

testifying of his gifts (v. 4)—Abel's offering proved something about his faith that was not demonstrated by Cain's offering.

Enoch (v. 5)—See Genesis 5:24. The LXX translated the Hebrew idiom "Enoch walked with God" with "he pleased God." The writer combines both in the reference. Enoch was miraculously taken to heaven without dying (see 1 Thess. 4:17).

impossible to please (v. 6)—Enoch pleased God because he had faith. Without such faith it is not possible for anyone to "walk with God" or "please Him" (see 10:38).

He is (v. 6)—The emphasis here is on "He," the true God. Genuine faith does not simply believe that a divine being exists, but that the God of Scripture is the only real and true God who exists. Not believing that God exists is equivalent to calling Him a liar (see 1 John 5:10).

rewarder (v. 6)—A person must believe not only that the true God exists, but also that He will reward men's faith in Him with forgiveness and righteousness, because He has promised to do so (see 10:35).

things not yet seen (v. 7)—The world had not seen anything resembling the great Flood (not even rain; see Gen. 7:11), yet Noah spent 120 years (Gen. 6:3) fulfilling God's command to build the massive ark (Gen. 6:13–22).

godly fear (v. 7)—Noah treated God's message with great respect and awe (see 5:7). His faith was expressed in obedience (see Gen. 6:22; 7:5).

condemned (v. 7)—Noah warned the people of his time about God's impending judgment (see 1 Pet. 3:20) and is called "a preacher of righteousness" (2 Pet. 2:5).

heir of the righteousness (v. 7)—See the notes on 6:12; 9:15. He who was a preacher of righteousness (2 Pet. 2:5) also became an heir of righteousness. He believed the message he preached. Like Enoch before him (see the notes on v. 5), Noah walked with God in faith and obedience (Gen. 6:9).

the place . . . inheritance (v. 8)—the land of Canaan, far from his original home in Ur of the Chaldees (Gen. 11:31); he went by faith

promise (v. 9)—Neither Abraham, Isaac, nor Jacob were able to settle permanently in or possess the land God promised to them (v. 10). Abraham first went there in faith, and they all lived there in faith, believing in a promise of possession that would not be fulfilled for many generations beyond their lifetimes (Gen. 12:7).

city (v. 10)—Abraham's ultimate and permanent Promised Land was heaven which, through faith, he knew he would ultimately inherit. This city is mentioned again in verse 16; 12:22; 13:14.

Sarah (vv. 11–12)—See Genesis 11:27–23:2; 1 Peter 3:5–6.

past the age (v. 11)—At ninety (Gen. 17:17), Sarah was long past child-bearing age and had never been able to conceive. God enabled her, however, because of her faith in His promise (Gen. 21:1–3).

as good as dead (v. 12)—At ninety-nine, Abraham was well beyond the age to father children apart from divine intervention (Gen. 17:1, 15–17; 21:1–5).

stars . . . sand (v. 12)—This is hyperbole to stress the vastness of the population that would come from Abraham's loins. See Genesis 15:4, 5; 22:17.

These all (v. 13)—The reference is to the patriarchs only (Abraham, Isaac, and Jacob). This interpretation is supported by the fact that the promises began with Abraham (see Gal. 3:14–18) and were passed on to Isaac (Gen. 26:2–5, 24) and Jacob (Gen. 28:10–15). In addition, only those individuals fit the description in verse 15, and Enoch did not die. See the note on 6:15. These people of faith didn't know when they would inherit the promise. They lived in the land but did not possess it.

strangers and pilgrims (vv. 13–16)—They were patient and endured great hardships because they believed God had something better. They had no desire to go back to Ur but did long for heaven (Job 19:25–26; Ps. 27:4).

their God (v. 16)—God referred to Himself as "the God of Abraham, the God of Isaac, and the God of Jacob" (Ex. 3:6; see Gen. 28:13; Matt. 22:32). This is a significant covenant formula whereby an individual or a people identified with God and He with them (see Lev. 26:12).

only begotten (vv. 17–18)—Isaac was not the only son of Abraham—there was also Ishmael by Hagar (Gen. 16:1–16) and other children by Keturah (25:1–4). The term refers to someone who is unique, one of a kind (see John 1:14). Isaac was the only son born according to God's promise and was the only heir of that promise. The quotation from Genesis 21:12 proves this latter point.

even from the dead (v. 19)—Believing that God's promise regarding Isaac was unconditional, Abraham came to the conclusion that God would fulfill that promise even if it required raising Isaac from the dead (see Gen. 22:5).

figurative sense (v. 19)—The word is the same as in 9:9, which is the basis for the English word parable. Abraham received Isaac back from the dead, as it were, even though Isaac had not been slain.

each of the sons (v. 21)—Both of Joseph's sons, Ephraim and Manasseh, received a blessing from Jacob. Consequently, two tribes descended from Joseph, whereas only one tribe descended from each of his brothers (see Gen. 47:31; 48:1, 5, 16).

top of his staff (v. 21)—According to Genesis 47:31, Jacob leaned upon his "bed." The two words (staff, bed) in Hebrew have exactly the same consonants. Old Testament Hebrew manuscripts were copied without vowels. Later Hebrew manuscripts, between the sixth and ninth centuries A.D., took the word as "bed." The LXX, in the third century B.C., rendered it "staff," which seems more likely, although both could be true.

Joseph (v. 22)—(See Gen. 37:1–50:26.) Joseph spent all of his adult life in Egypt and, even though he was a fourth-generation heir of the promise given to Abraham, he never returned to Canaan while he was alive. Yet, facing death, he still had faith that God would fulfill His promise and demonstrated that confidence by making his brothers promise to take his bones back to Canaan for burial (Gen. 50:24–25; see Ex. 13:19; Josh. 24:32).

beautiful child (v. 23)—Meaning "favored," in this case divinely favored (Acts 7:20; see Ex. 2:2). The faith described here is actually that exercised by Moses' parents, although it is unclear how much Moses' parents understood about God's plan for their child.

with the people of God (v. 25)—Moses would have sinned had he refused to take on the responsibility God gave him regarding Israel, and he had a clear and certain conviction that "God would deliver them by his hand" (Acts 7:25). Moses repudiated the pleasures of Egypt.

reproach of Christ (v. 26)—Moses suffered reproach for the sake of Christ in the sense that he identified with Messiah's people in their suffering (v. 25). In addition, Moses identified himself with the Messiah because of his own role as leader and prophet (see 12:2; Deut. 18:15; Ps. 69:9; 89:51). Moses knew of the sufferings and glory of the Messiah (see John 5:46; Acts 26:22, 23; 1 Pet. 1:10–12). Anyone who suffers because of genuine faith in God and for the redemptive gospel suffers for the sake of Christ (see 13:12–13; 1 Pet. 4:14).

forsook Egypt (v. 27)—Moses left Egypt for the first time when he fled for his life after killing the Egyptian slave master (Ex. 2:14–15). That time he did fear Pharaoh's wrath. On the second occasion, he turned his back on Egypt and all that it represented. This leaving was not for fear of Pharaoh, so it is the one in view here.

seeing Him (v. 27)—Moses's faith was such that he responded to God's commands as though God were standing visibly before him. This was the basis for his loyalty to God, and it should be a believer's example for loyalty.

Red Sea (v. 29)—See Exodus 14, 15. When they first reached the shores of the Red Sea, the people feared for their lives (Ex. 14:11, 21). But upon hearing Moses's pronouncement of God's protection (Ex. 14:13–14), they went forward in faith.

Jericho (v. 30)—See Joshua 6. The people did nothing militarily to cause the fall of Jericho; they simply followed God's instructions in faith. See 2 Corinthians 10:4.

David (v. 32)—David is the only king mentioned in this verse. All the others are judges or prophets. David could also be considered a prophet (see 1 Samuel 13:14; 16:1, 12; 2 Sam. 23:1–3; Mark 12:36; Acts 13:22; Heb. 4:7).

Samuel and the prophets (v. 32)—Samuel was the last of the judges and the first of the prophets (see 1 Samuel 7:15; Acts 3:24; 13:20). He anointed David as king (1 Samuel 16:13) and was known as a man of intercessory prayer (1 Samuel 12:19, 23; Jer. 15:1).

subdued kingdoms (v. 33)—Joshua, the judges, David, and others

worked righteousness (v. 33)—righteous kings like David, Solomon, Asa, Jehoshaphat, Joash, Hezekiah, and Josiah

obtained promises (v. 33)—Abraham, Moses, David, and Solomon

stopped the mouths of lions (v. 33)—Samson (Judg. 14:5–6), David (1 Samuel 17:34–35), and Daniel (Dan. 6:22)

quenched the violence of fire (v. 34)—Shadrach, Meshach, and Abednego (Dan. 3:19–30)

escaped the edge of the sword (v. 34)—David (1 Samuel 18:4, 11; 19:9, 10), Elijah (1 Kin. 19:1–3, 10), and Elisha (2 Kin. 6:15–19).

weakness (v. 34)—Ehud (Judg. 3:12–30), Jael (Judg. 4:17–24), Gideon (Judg. 6:15, 16; 7:1–25), Samson (Judg. 16:21–30), and Hezekiah (Is. 38:1–6); (see 1 Cor. 1:27; 2 Cor. 12:10).

Women received their dead (v. 35)—the widow of Zarephath (1Kin. 17:22) and the woman of Shunem (2 Kin. 4:34)

tortured (v. 35)—The word indicates that they were beaten to death while strapped to some sort of rack.

better resurrection (v. 35)—See the note on 9:27. The deliverance from certain death or near death would be like returning from the dead, but would not be the promised resurrection. This was especially true of those who had died and were raised. The first time they were raised from the dead was merely resuscitation, not the true and glorious final resurrection (Dan. 12:2; see Matt. 5:10; James 1:12).

others (v. 36)—Joseph (Gen. 39:20), Micaiah (1Kin. 22:27), Elisha (2 Kin. 2:23), Hanani (2 Chr. 16:10), Jeremiah (Jer. 20:1–6; 37:15), and others (2 Chr. 36:16)

stoned (v. 37)—The prophet Zechariah (son of Jehoiada) was killed in this fashion (see the notes on 2 Chr. 24:20–22; see Introduction to Zechariah: Author and Date).

sawn in two (v. 37)—According to tradition, this was the method Manasseh employed to execute Isaiah.

slain with the sword (v. 37)—Uriah the prophet died in this fashion (Jer. 26:23; see 1Kin. 19:10). However, the expression here may refer to the mass execution of God's people; several such incidents occurred during the time of the Maccabees in the four hundred years between the Old Testament and New Testament.

wandered about (v. 37)—Many of God's people suffered from poverty and persecution (see Ps. 107:4–9).

something better (vv. 39–40)—They had faith in the ultimate fulfillment of the eternal promises in the covenant (v. 13). See Introduction: Historical and Theological Themes.

apart from us (v. 40)—The faith of Old Testament saints looked forward to the promised salvation, whereas the faith of those after Christ looks back to the fulfillment of the promise. Both groups are characterized by genuine faith and are saved by Christ's atoning work on the cross (see Eph. 2:8–9).

Understanding the Text

4) In 10:19–25, the writer of Hebrews lists some marks that will be evident in the lives of those who respond positively to the gospel. What are they?

_____

_____

_____

5) How is apostasy described in 10:26–39? What consequences are listed? What deterrents are listed in verses 32–36?

_____

_____

_____

6) What is faith (that is, how is it described and pictured in chapter 11)?

_____

_____

_____

7) Each time the phrase "by faith" is used in chapter 11, it is followed by a description of the actions taken by the individuals who acted in that faith.

Go back through the chapter and circle the verbs that describe how these "Heroes of Faith" lived out the "substance of things hoped for" (v. 1). Then read through the chapter again and underline the phrases that explain why they did these things. What do you learn about faith and how is your view of God expanded by these observations?

_____

_____

_____

Cross-Reference

Read James 2:14–26.

14 *What does it profit, my brethren, if someone says he has faith but does not have works? Can faith save him?*

15 *If a brother or sister is naked and destitute of daily food,*

16 *and one of you says to them, "Depart in peace, be warmed and filled," but you do not give them the things which are needed for the body, what does it profit?*

17 *Thus also faith by itself, if it does not have works, is dead.*

18 *But someone will say, "You have faith, and I have works." Show me your faith without your works, and I will show you my faith by my works.*

19 *You believe that there is one God. You do well. Even the demons believe—and tremble!*

20 *But do you want to know, O foolish man, that faith without works is dead?*

21 *Was not Abraham our father justified by works when he offered Isaac his son on the altar?*

22 *Do you see that faith was working together with his works, and by works faith was made perfect?*

23 *And the Scripture was fulfilled which says, "Abraham believed God, and it was accounted to him for righteousness." And he was called the friend of God.*

24 *You see then that a man is justified by works, and not by faith only.*

25 *Likewise, was not Rahab the harlot also justified by works when she received the messengers and sent them out another way?*

26 *For as the body without the spirit is dead, so faith without works is dead also.*

8) What additional insights does this passage from James shed on the subject of faith? How does this tie in with what Hebrews 11 portrays?

_____

_____

_____

Exploring the Meaning

9) Read Habakkuk 2:3–4. What does this passage mean and how does it relate to Hebrews 11?

_____

_____

_____

(verses to consider: Rom. 1:17; Eph. 2:8; Col. 2:6)

10) Read Deuteronomy 4:29. In what ways does God reward those who seek Him?

_____

_____

_____

(verses to consider: Gen. 15:1; 1 Chr. 28:9; Ps. 58:11; Is. 40:10)

11) Read 2 Corinthians 4:16–18. How is this passage a good description of faith?

_____

_____

_____

Summing Up . . .

"There was once a young boy whose dad left him on a downtown corner one morning and told him to wait there until he returned in about half an hour. But the father's car broke down and he could not get to a phone. Five hours went by before the father managed to get back, and he was worried that his son would be in a state of panic. But when the father got there, the boy was standing in front of the dime store, looking in the window and rocking back and forth on his heels. When the father saw him, he ran up to him and threw his arms around him and hugged and kissed him. The father apologized and said, 'Weren't you worried? Did you think I was never coming back?' The boy looked up and replied, 'No, Dad. I knew you were coming. You said you would.'

"God's answers may seem to be a long time in coming, and our waiting may be uncomfortable or even painful. But He will always do just as He has said He will do. The reason we can hold fast to our hope without wavering is that He who promised is faithful."—John MacArthur, *Hebrews*, Moody Press, 1983, p. 267.

Reflecting on the Text

12) If you could be one of the characters in Hebrews 11 for one day, which character would you pick and why?

_____

_____

_____

13) How would you rate your trust in God on a scale of 1–10 (with 1 being "pitiful" and 10 being "powerful")? What concrete yet risky steps could you take to demonstrate a more radical faith?

_____

_____

_____

14) In what ways have you made this world your home? What two specific actions could you start doing or stop doing to live more like a "stranger and pilgrim" in the world?

_____

_____

_____

_____

_____

_____

Recording Your Thoughts

_____

_____

_____

_____

_____

_____

_____

_____

_____

_____

_____

For further study, see the following passages:

Genesis 23:4	Deuteronomy 17:2–7	Psalms 15; 73:28; 135:4
Isaiah 26:11	Zephaniah 1:18	Matthew 12:31;
John 6:29; 14:6	Acts 5:41; 7:17; 9:2	Romans 4:13; 12:19
1 Corinthians 4:9	Ephesians 2:8–9; 5:25–26	Galatians 2:20
2 Thessalonians 1:7–9	2 Timothy 2:5	Titus 3:5
James 1:2; 4:8		

Perseverance

Opening Thought

1) What is your favorite sport in which to participate? How about to watch?

_____

_____

_____

_____

2) How were you disciplined when you were young?

_____

_____

_____

_____

3) What trials in your life have been the most difficult and why?

_____

_____

_____

4) How does a person become bitter? (that is, what is the process?)

_____

_____

_____

Background of the Passage

The background of the Book of Hebrews is a climate of persecution. The Jews to whom the Book of Hebrews was written were targeted for abuse because of their break with Judaism. The harassment was coming from their Jewish friends and relatives who resented their turning their backs on the religious customs and traditions in which they had been born and raised. Even the unregenerate Jews who were involved with the church must have suffered because of their association with Christians.

The affliction had largely been in the form of social and economic pressure, though some of them had been imprisoned (10:34). Surely many of these believers were wondering why, if their God was a God of power and of peace, they were suffering so much. "Where is the God who is supposed to supply all our needs and give us the answers to our questions and fulfillment to our lives? Why, when we turned to a God of love, did everyone start hating us?"

Chapter 12 is a strong call to perseverance. It admonishes weary believers to "run with endurance" the "race" that is the Christian life (vv. 1–3). It reminds wavering believers that God uses hardship and affliction as a means of discipline, as a means of training His children and helping them mature (vv. 4–11). It exhorts struggling believers to continue diligently and vigilantly in the faith (vv. 12–17). Finally, it warns fearful believers not to fear men more than God (vv. 18–29), for He is "a consuming fire."

If you are struggling or tempted to throw in the towel on your faith, this study is for you!

Bible Passage

Read 12:1–29, noting the key words and definitions to the right of the passage.

Hebrews 12:1–29

1 *Therefore we also, since we are surrounded by so great a cloud of witnesses, let us lay aside every weight, and the sin which so easily ensnares us, and let us run with endurance the race that is set before us,*

2 *looking unto Jesus, the author and finisher of our faith, who for the joy that was set before Him*

Therefore (v. 1)—This is a very crucial transition word offering an emphatic conclusion to the section which began in 10:19.

witnesses (v. 1)—The deceased people of chapter 11 give witness to the value and blessing of living by faith. Motivation for running "the race" is not in the possibility of receiving praise from "observing"

endured the cross, despising the shame, and has sat down at the right hand of the throne of God.

3 For consider Him who endured such hostility from sinners against Himself, lest you become weary and discouraged in your souls.

4 You have not yet resisted to bloodshed, striving against sin.

5 And you have forgotten the exhortation which speaks to you as to sons:

"My son, do not despise the chastening of the LORD,

Nor be discouraged when you are rebuked by Him;

6 For whom the LORD loves He chastens,

And scourges every son whom He receives."

7 If you endure chastening, God deals with you as with sons; for what son is there whom a father does not chasten?

8 But if you are without chastening, of which all have become partakers, then you are illegitimate and not sons.

9 Furthermore, we have had human fathers who corrected us, and we paid them respect. Shall we not much more readily be in subjection to the Father of spirits and live?

10 For they indeed for a few days chastened us as seemed best to them, but He for our profit, that we may be partakers of His holiness.

11 Now no chastening seems to be joyful for the present, but painful; nevertheless, afterward it yields the peaceable fruit of righteousness to those who have been trained by it.

12 Therefore strengthen the hands which hang down, and the feeble knees,

13 and make straight paths for your feet, so that what is lame may not be dislocated, but rather be healed.

14 Pursue peace with all people, and holiness, without which no one will see the Lord:

15 looking carefully lest anyone fall short of the

heavenly saints. Rather, the runner is inspired by the godly examples those saints set during their lives. The great crowd is not spectators but is composed of ones whose past lives of faith encourage others to live that way (see 11:2, 4–5, 33, 39).

let us (v. 1)—The reference is to those Hebrews who had made a profession of Christ, but had not gone all the way to full faith. They had not yet begun the race, which starts with salvation. The writer has invited them to accept salvation in Christ and join the race.

every weight (v. 1)—Different from the "sin" mentioned next, this refers to the main encumbrance weighing down the Hebrews, which was the Levitical system with its stifling legalism. The athlete would strip away every piece of unnecessary clothing before competing in the race. The outward things emphasized by the Levitical system not only impede, they "ensnare."

sin (v. 1)—In this context, this focuses first on the particular sin of unbelief—refusing to turn away from the Levitical sacrifices to the perfect sacrifice, Jesus Christ (see John 16:8–11), as well as other sins cherished by the unbeliever.

endurance (v. 1)—Endurance is the steady determination to keep going, regardless of the temptation to slow down or give up (see 1 Cor. 9:24, 25).

race (v. 1)—The athletic metaphor presents the faith-filled life as a demanding, grueling effort. The English word agony is derived from the Greek word used here. See Matt. 7:14.

looking (v. 2)—They were to fix their eyes on Jesus as the object of faith and salvation (see 11:26–27; Acts 7:55, 56; Phil. 3:8).

author (v. 2)—See the note on 2:10. The term means "originator" or "preeminent example".

grace of God; lest any root of bitterness springing up cause trouble, and by this many become defiled;

16 lest there be any fornicator or profane person like Esau, who for one morsel of food sold his birthright.

17 For you know that afterward, when he wanted to inherit the blessing, he was rejected, for he found no place for repentance, though he sought it diligently with tears.

18 For you have not come to the mountain that may be touched and that burned with fire, and to blackness and darkness and tempest,

19 and the sound of a trumpet and the voice of words, so that those who heard it begged that the word should not be spoken to them anymore.

20 (For they could not endure what was commaned: "And if so much as a beast touches the mountain, it shall be stoned or shot with an arrow."

21 And so terrifying was the sight that Moses said, "I am exceedingly afraid and trembling.")

22 But you have come to Mount Zion and to the city of the living God, the heavenly Jerusalem, to an innumerable company of angels,

23 to the general assembly and church of the firstborn who are registered in heaven, to God the Judge of all, to the spirits of just men made perfect,

24 to Jesus the Mediator of the new covenant, and to the blood of sprinkling that speaks better things than that of Abel.

25 See that you do not refuse Him who speaks. For if they did not escape who refused Him who spoke on earth, much more shall we not escape if we turn away from Him who speaks from heaven,

26 whose voice then shook the earth; but now He has promised, saying, "Yet once more I shake not only the earth, but also heaven."

27 Now this, "Yet once more," indicates the removal

finisher (v. 2)—See the note on 5:14. The term is literally "perfecter," having the idea of carrying through to perfect completion (see John 19:30).

the joy (v. 2)—Jesus persevered so that He might receive the joy of accomplishment of the Father's will and exaltation (see 1:9; Ps. 16:9–11 Luke 10:21–24).

right hand (v. 2)—See the note on 1:3.

consider Him (v. 3)—Jesus is the supreme example of willingness to suffer in obedience to God. He faced "hostility" (the same word as "spoken against" in Luke 2:34) and endured even the cruel cross. The same opposition is faced by all who follow Him (Acts 28:22; Gal. 6:17; Col. 1:24; 2 Tim. 3:12).

weary and discouraged (v. 3) —Believers' pressures, exhaustion, and persecutions (see Gal. 6:9) are as nothing compared to Christ's.

bloodshed (v. 4)—None of the Hebrews had experienced such intense exhaustion or persecution that it brought them to death or martyrdom. Since Stephen (Acts 7:60), James (Acts 12:1), and others (see Acts 9:1; 22:4; 26:10) had faced martyrdom in Jerusalem, it would appear to rule out that city as the residence of this epistle's recipients (see Introduction: Author and Date).

scourges (v. 6)—This refers to flogging with a whip, a severe and painful form of beating that was a common Jewish practice (see Matt. 10:17; 23:34).

sons (vv. 7–8)—Because all are imperfect and need discipline and training, all true children of God are chastened at one time or another, in one way or another.

illegitimate (v. 8)—The word is found only here in the New Testament, but is used elsewhere in Greek literature of those born to

of those things that are being shaken, as of things that are made, that the things which cannot be shaken may remain.

28 *Therefore, since we are receiving a kingdom which cannot be shaken, let us have grace, by which we may serve God acceptably with reverence and godly fear.*

29 *For our God is a consuming fire.*

slaves or concubines. There could be in this an implied reference to Hagar and Ishmael (Gen. 16), Abraham's concubine and illegitimate son.

subjection (v. 9)—Respect for God equals submission to His will and law, and those who willingly receive the Lord's chastening will have a richer, more abundant life (see Ps. 119:165).

Father of spirits (v. 9)— Probably best translated as "Father of our spirits," it is in contrast to "human fathers" (literally "fathers of our flesh").

our profit (v. 10)—Imperfect human fathers discipline imperfectly; but God is perfect and therefore His discipline is perfect and always for the spiritual good of His children.

fruit of righteousness (v. 11)— This is the same phrase as in James 3:18.

trained (v. 11)—The same word was used in 5:14 and translated "exercised" (see the note there; see 1 Tim. 4:17).

Pursue . . . holiness (v. 14)—In this epistle, it is explained as (1) a drawing near to God with full faith and a cleansed conscience (10:14, 22), and (2) a genuine acceptance of Christ as the Savior and sacrifice for sin, bringing the sinner into fellowship with God. Unbelievers will not be drawn to accept Christ if believers' lives do not demonstrate the qualities God desires, including peace and holiness (see John 13:35; 1 Tim. 4:3; 5:23; 1 Pet. 1:16).

looking carefully (v. 15)— Believers are to watch their own lives, so as to give a testimony of peace and holiness, as well as to look out for and help those in their midst who are in need of salvation.

fall short of the grace of God (v. 15)—See the notes on 4:1; 6:6; 10:26. This means to come too late and be left out. Here is another mention of the intellectually convinced Jews in that assembly, who knew the gospel and were drawn to Christ, but still stood on the edge of apostasy.

root of bitterness (v. 15)—This is the attitude of unbelievers within the church who are corrupting influences. See Deuteronomy 29:18.

fornicator (v. 16)—In this context, it refers to the sexually immoral in general. Apostasy is often closely linked with immorality (see 2 Pet. 2:10, 14, 18; Jude 8, 16, 18).

Mount Zion (v. 22)—As opposed to Mount Sinai, where God gave the Mosaic law which was forbidding and terrifying, Mount Zion here is not the earthly one in Jerusalem but God's heavenly abode, which is inviting and gracious. No one could please God on Sinai's terms, which was perfect fulfillment of the law (Gal. 3:10–12). Zion, however, is accessible to all who come to God through Jesus Christ (see Ps. 132:13–14; Is. 46:13; Zech. 2:10; Gal. 4:21–31).

Mount Zion . . . city of the living God . . . heavenly Jerusalem (v. 22)—These are synonyms for heaven itself. For a description of the abode of God, the city of Jerusalem in heaven, see Revelation 21:1–22:5.

innumerable (v. 22)—The Greek word is often translated ten thousand (see Rev. 5:11–12).

general assembly (v. 23)—The term here means "a gathering for public festival." It does not likely describe distinct group as if different from the church, but describes the attitude of the innumerable angels in heaven in a festal gathering around the throne of God.

church of the firstborn (v. 23)—The firstborn is Jesus Christ (see the note on 1:6). The "church" is comprised of believers who are fellow heirs with Christ, the preeminent One among many brethren (Rom. 8:17, 29).

just men made perfect (v. 23)—These are the Old Testament saints in distinction from the "church of the firstborn," who are the New Testament believers.

better things (v. 24)—Abel's sacrifice was pleasing to God because it was offered in faith and obedience (see 11:4), but it had no atoning power. Jesus' blood alone was sufficient to cleanse sin (see 1 John 1:7). The sacrifice of Christ brought redemption (9:12), forgiveness (9:26), and complete salvation (10:10, 14).

than that of Abel (v. 24)—The blood of Abel's sacrifice only provided a temporary covering, but Christ's blood sacrifice declares eternal forgiveness (see Col. 1:20).

refused (v. 25)—See the note on verse 19, where the same word describes the conduct of the Israelites at Mount Sinai.

much more (v. 25)—The consequences for apostates is dire indeed. The judgment to be experienced and the expected terror is far in excess of that on Mount Sinai.

shook the earth (vv. 26–27)—At Mount Sinai, God shook the earth. From Zion, He will shake the heavens and the entire universe (see Is. 13:13; 34:4; 65:17, 22; 2 Pet. 3:10–13; Rev. 6:12–14; 20:11; 21:1).

kingdom (v. 28)—God will create "a new heaven and a new earth . . . the holy city, New Jerusalem" (Rev. 21:1–2), which will be eternal and immovable.

with reverence and godly fear (v. 28)—The second word has to do with the apprehension felt due to being in God's presence.

consuming fire (v. 29)—God's law given at Sinai prescribed many severe punishments, but the punishment is far worse for those who reject His offer of salvation through His own Son, Jesus Christ (see Luke 3:16–17). This verse is to be related to 10:29–31.

Understanding the Text

5) What kind of example is set by the "great cloud of witnesses" and by Jesus (in vv. 2–4)? Why did the writer of Hebrews point his readers to these examples?

_____

_____

6) Why is running a foot race a good metaphor for the Christian life? What other analogies are used in the New Testament?

_____

_____

(verses to consider: 1 Cor. 9:24–26; Gal. 5:7; Eph. 6:11–17; 2 Tim. 2:3–7; 4:6–8)

7) What does 12:4–11 teach about divine discipline—its purposes, prevention, and perils, as well as what it proves?

_____

_____

8) What strong exhortations are given in 12:12–17?

_____

_____

(verses to consider: Prov. 4:25–27; Rom. 12:18; 1 John 2:6)

9) How and why are Mount Sinai and Mount Zion contrasted in this passage?

_____

_____

(verses to consider: Ex. 20:18–19; Ps. 132:13–14; 133:3)

Cross-Reference

Read Psalm 42.

To the Chief Musician. A Contemplation of the sons of Korah.
1 *As the deer pants for the water brooks,*
So pants my soul for You, O God.
2 *My soul thirsts for God, for the living God.*
When shall I come and appear before God?
3 *My tears have been my food day and night,*
While they continually say to me,
"Where is your God?"
4 *When I remember these things,*
I pour out my soul within me.
For I used to go with the multitude;
I went with them to the house of God,
With the voice of joy and praise,
With a multitude that kept a pilgrim feast.
5 *Why are you cast down, O my soul?*
And why are you disquieted within me?
Hope in God, for I shall yet praise Him
For the help of His countenance.
6 *O my God, my soul is cast down within me;*
Therefore I will remember You from the land of the Jordan,
And from the heights of Hermon,
From the Hill Mizar.
7 *Deep calls unto deep at the noise of Your waterfalls;*
All Your waves and billows have gone over me.
8 *The* LORD *will command His lovingkindness in the daytime,*
And in the night His song shall be with me—
A prayer to the God of my life.
9 *I will say to God my Rock,*
"Why have You forgotten me?
Why do I go mourning because of the oppression of the enemy?"
10 *As with a breaking of my bones,*
My enemies reproach me,
While they say to me all day long,
"Where is your God?"
11 *Why are you cast down, O my soul?*
And why are you disquieted within me?
Hope in God;
For I shall yet praise Him,
The help of my countenance and my God.

10) How does this Old Testament passage illustrate the various truths taught in Hebrews 12?

_____

_____

Exploring the Meaning

11) Verse 2 says that Jesus endured the cross for the "joy that was set before Him." Read Psalm 16:9–11. What part does (or should) joy play in our lives as we seek to live for Christ and His glory?

_____

_____

(verses to consider: Matt. 25:21; Phil. 2:17; 4:1)

12) Read Proverbs 13:24. What does this say about love and discipline? How does this relate to Hebrews 12?

_____

_____

Summing Up . . .

"Endurance is steady determination to keep going. It means continuing even when everything in you wants to slow down or give up. I can still remember the excruciating experience I had in high school when I first ran the half-mile. I was used to the hundred-yard dash, which requires more speed but is over quickly. So I started out well; in fact I led the pack for the first hundred yards or so. But I ended dead last, and almost felt I was dead. My legs were wobbly, my chest was heaving, my mouth was cottony, and I collapsed at the finish line. That is the way many people live the Christian life. They start out fast, but as the race goes on they slow down, give up, or just collapse. The Christian race is a marathon, a long-distance race, not a sprint. The church has always had many short-spurt Christians, but the Lord wants those who will 'make the distance.' There will be obstacles and there will be weariness and exhaustion, but we must endure if we are to win. God is concerned for steadfastness."—John MacArthur, *Hebrews*, Moody Press, 1983, p. 373.

Reflecting on the Text

13) Discipline is an important practice to develop. From the demanding coach in a grueling practice to the pruning back of a rose bush in a garden, it's discipline that ultimately causes growth.

In what areas of your life do you sense God has been or is disciplining you? Why?

_____

_____

14) What are some specific encumbrances and entangling sins that you need to be on the lookout for this week?

_____

_____

15) If you are a Christian, you have "come to Mount Zion and the city of the living God, the heavenly Jerusalem." How often do you think about heaven and that you are already considered a citizen of heaven (Phil. 3:20)? What are some specific, practical things you can do to focus more on heaven each day? What needs to change so that your life better reflects your citizenship?

_____

_____

Recording Your Thoughts

_____

_____

For further study, see the following passages:

Genesis 25:29–34	Genesis 27:1–39	Exodus 19
Deuteronomy 4:10–24	Deuteronomy 5:22–24	Deuteronomy 9:19
Proverbs 3:11–12; 4:25–27	Isaiah 35:3; 54:10; 63:9	Lamentations 3:31–33
Ezekiel 18:32	Haggai 2:6	Luke 10:20
Romans 8:29	1 Corinthians 11:30	2 Corinthians 12:7–10
Galatians 2:10; 4:19	1 John 5:16	

Christian Behavior

Opening Thought

1) What your standard or customary way of concluding your letters? If someone were sending you vital information, would you prefer to get it via e-mail, "snail mail," phone call, or fax? Why?

_____

_____

_____

_____

2) Many unbelievers claim they are not interested in Christianity because of the hypocritical behavior of believers. In your opinion, to what extent is this a valid excuse or simply a smoke screen?

_____

_____

_____

_____

3) What are the pros and cons of concentrating on doing good works?

_____

_____

_____

_____

_____

Background of the Passage

"The world," said Alexander Maclaren, "takes its notion of God most of all from those who say they belong to God's family. They read us a great deal more than they read the Bible. They see us; they only hear about Jesus Christ."

Unfortunately, throughout the history of the church, the mean, prejudiced, and immoral lives of professed Christians have given the world a ready excuse to malign the claims of Christ. Perhaps this phenomenon explains the rationale for Hebrews 13.

The first 11 chapters of Hebrews do not emphasize specific commands to Christians. There is an obvious lack of practical explanations or exhortations. The bulk of the book is pure doctrine and is almost entirely directed to Jews who had received the gospel but who needed to be affirmed in the superiority of the New Covenant.

The exhortations in chapter 12 that apply to Christians are general, encouraging them to endure and to pursue righteousness. The specific practical exhortations for Christians are in chapter 13. This fits the pattern of New Testament teaching, which is always doctrine and then duty, beliefs then behavior, position and then practice. Chapter 13 is not an afterthought; it is integral to the message of the book. A pure faith demands a pure life.

Chapter 13 gives some of the essential practical ethics of Christian living that help portray the true gospel to the world, that encourage men to trust in Christ, and that bring glory to God.

Bible Passage

Read 13:1–25, noting the key words and definitions to the right of the passage.

Hebrews 13:1–25

¹ Let brotherly love continue.

² Do not forget to entertain strangers, for by so doing some have unwittingly entertained angels.

³ Remember the prisoners as if chained with them—those who are mistreated—since you yourselves are in the body also.

⁴ Marriage is honorable among all, and the bed

entertain (v. 2)—The second grace needing development was the extension of love to those who were strangers. Hospitality in the ancient world often included putting up a guest overnight or longer. This is hardest to do when experiencing a time of persecution. The Hebrews would not know whether a guest would prove to be a spy or a fellow believer being pursued.

undefiled; but fornicators and adulterers God will judge.

5 Let your conduct be without covetousness; be content with such things as you have. For He Himself has said, "I will never leave you nor forsake you."

6 So we may boldly say:
"The LORD is my helper;
I will not fear.
What can man do to me?"

7 Remember those who rule over you, who have spoken the word of God to you, whose faith follow, considering the outcome of their conduct.

8 Jesus Christ is the same yesterday, today, and forever.

9 Do not be carried about with various and strange doctrines. For it is good that the heart be established by grace, not with foods which have not profited those who have been occupied with them.

10 We have an altar from which those who serve the tabernacle have no right to eat.

11 For the bodies of those animals, whose blood is brought into the sanctuary by the high priest for sin, are burned outside the camp.

12 Therefore Jesus also, that He might sanctify the people with His own blood, suffered outside the gate.

13 Therefore let us go forth to Him, outside the camp, bearing His reproach.

14 For here we have no continuing city, but we seek the one to come.

15 Therefore by Him let us continually offer the sacrifice of praise to God, that is, the fruit of our lips, giving thanks to His name.

16 But do not forget to do good and to share, for with such sacrifices God is well pleased.

17 Obey those who rule over you, and be submissive, for they watch out for your souls, as those who must give account. Let them do so with joy and not with grief, for that would be unprofitable for you.

angels (v. 2)—This is not given as the ultimate motivation for hospitality but to reveal that one never knows how far reaching an act of kindness might be. This is exactly what happened to Abraham and Sarah (Gen. 18:1–3), Lot (Gen. 19:1–2), Gideon (Judg. 6:11–24), and Manoah (Judg. 13:6–20).

yourselves. (v. 3)—Believers should be able to identify with the suffering of others because they also suffer physical ("in the body") pain and hardship.

honorable (v. 4)—God highly honors marriage, which He instituted at creation (Gen. 2:24); but some people in the early church considered celibacy to be holier than marriage, an idea Paul strongly denounces in 1 Timothy 4:3 (see also 1 Cor. 7). Sexual activity in a marriage is pure, but any sexual activity outside marriage brings one under divine judgment.

God will judge (v. 4)—God prescribes serious consequences for sexual immorality.

covetousness (v. 5)—Lusting after material riches is "a root of all kinds of evil, for which some have strayed from the faith in their greediness" (1 Tim. 6:10; see 1 Tim. 3:3).

I will never (v. 5)—Believers can be content in every situation because of this promise. Five negatives are utilized in this statement to emphasize the impossibility of Christ deserting believers. It is like saying "there is absolutely no way whatsoever that I will ever, ever leave you."

boldly (v. 6)—Not the usual word for boldness, this word has the idea of being confident and courageous (see its use in Matt. 9:2; 2 Corinthians 5:6, 8).

Remember those who rule over you (v. 7)—In addition to the roll of the faithful in chapter 11, the writer reminds the Hebrews of their own faithful leaders within the church. In so doing, he outlines

¹⁸ *Pray for us; for we are confident that we have a good conscience, in all things desiring to live honorably.*

¹⁹ *But I especially urge you to do this, that I may be restored to you the sooner.*

²⁰ *Now may the God of peace who brought up our Lord Jesus from the dead, that great Shepherd of the sheep, through the blood of the everlasting covenant,*

²¹ *make you complete in every good work to do His will, working in you what is well pleasing in His sight, through Jesus Christ, to whom be glory forever and ever. Amen.*

²² *And I appeal to you, brethren, bear with the word of exhortation, for I have written to you in few words.*

²³ *Know that our brother Timothy has been set free, with whom I shall see you if he comes shortly.*

²⁴ *Greet all those who rule over you, and all the saints. Those from Italy greet you.*

²⁵ *Grace be with you all. Amen.*

the duties of pastors: (1) rule; (2) speak the Word of God; and (3) establish the pattern of faith for the people to follow (see 1 Tim. 3:1–7).

various and strange doctrines (v. 9)—These would include any teaching contrary to God's Word. The New Testament contains countless warnings against false teaching and false teachers (see Acts 20:29–30; Rom. 16:17; 2 Corinthians 10:4–5).

established by grace (v. 9)—Those who are experiencing God's grace in Christ have hearts and minds that remain stable.

foods (v. 9)—The Mosaic law had regulations for everything, including food (Lev. 11). But for Christians, those laws have been abrogated (Acts 10:9–16).

an altar (v. 10)—The altar, the offerer, and the sacrifice are all closely related. Association with an altar identifies the offerer with the sacrifice. With certain offerings, the individual further identified himself with the altar and sacrifice by eating some of the sacrifice. The apostle Paul referred to this relationship to an altar when giving instruction to the Corinthians regarding eating meat offered to idols (1 Cor. 9:13) and regarding the observation of the Lord's Supper (1 Cor. 10:18). Here, the altar is equivalent to the sacrifice of Christ, especially as seen in the comparison to the Day of Atonement.

praise . . . thanks (v. 15)—As seen throughout the Book of Hebrews, sacrifices were extremely important under the Old Covenant. Under the New Covenant, God desires the praise and thanksgiving of His people rather than offerings of animals or grain. Since New Testament believers are all priests, they have offerings of praise and thanks to God.

do good . . . share (v. 16)—The sacrifices of praise coming from the lips of God's people please Him only when accompanied by loving action (see Is. 58:6–7).

rule over you (v. 17)—See the note on verse 7. The pastors/elders of the church exercise the very authority of Christ when they preach, teach, and apply Scripture correctly. They serve the church on behalf of Christ and must give Him an account of their faithfulness. These may include both secular and spiritual rulers. Even those who do not acknowledge God are nevertheless ordained and used by Him (see Rom. 13:1, 4).

joy (v. 17)—The church is responsible to help its leaders do their work with satisfaction and delight (see 1 Thess. 5:12–13).

restored (v. 19)—The author had been with these Hebrews and was anxious to once again be in their fellowship.

Now (v. 20)—This benediction is among the most beautiful in Scripture. It is an example of how grace can be manifested in mutual blessing and prayer.

God of peace (v. 20)—Paul uses this title six times in his epistles (see 1 Thess. 5:23).

great Shepherd of the sheep (v. 20)—The figure of the Messiah as a Shepherd is found frequently in Scripture (see Ps. 23; Is. 40:11; Ezek. 34:23; John 10:11; 1 Pet. 2:25).

through the blood of the everlasting covenant (v. 20)—This must refer, in the context of Hebrews, to the New Covenant that is eternal (in a future sense) compared to the Mosaic Covenant that was temporary and had been abrogated (see the notes on 8:6–13; 9:15).

make you complete (v. 21)—This is not the Greek word for "perfect" or "perfection" used throughout Hebrews to indicate salvation (see the note on 5:14) but is a word which is translated "prepared" in 10:5 and "framed" in 11:3. It refers to believers being edified. The verb has the idea of equipping by means of adjusting, shaping, mending, restoring, or preparing (see 1 Cor. 1:10; 2 Corinthians 13:11; 2 Tim. 3:17).

bear with (v. 22)—Readers are encouraged to receive this message with open minds and warm hearts, in contrast to those who "will not endure sound doctrine" (2 Tim. 4:3).

word of exhortation (v. 22)—This is the writer's own description of his epistle (see Introduction: Historical and Theological Themes).

set free (v. 23)—The details of Timothy's imprisonment are unknown (see 2 Tim. 4:11, 21).

Understanding the Text

Go through the passage and circle each of the commands given in this chapter.

4) What words about marriage and sexual purity are found here?

_____

_____

(verses to consider: Gen. 2:24; Prov. 5:1–23; Eph. 5:3–6)

5) What does this chapter teach about God's presence?

(verses to consider: Deut. 31:6, 8; Josh. 1:5; 1 Chr. 28:20)

6) How is "the sacrifice of praise" defined in this passage? What other sacrifices please God (v. 16)?

_____

_____

7) What commands are given to believers regarding submitting to spiritual leadership in the church?

_____

_____

(vv. to consider: 1 Cor. 4:1–5; 1 Thess. 5:12–13; 1 Pet. 5:1–4)

Cross-Reference

Read 1 Thessalonians 4:1–12.

¹ *Finally then, brethren, we urge and exhort in the Lord Jesus that you should abound more and more, just as you received from us how you ought to walk and to please God;*

² *for you know what commandments we gave you through the Lord Jesus.*

³ *For this is the will of God, your sanctification: that you should abstain from sexual immorality;*

⁴ *that each of you should know how to possess his own vessel in sanctification and honor,*

⁵ *not in passion of lust, like the Gentiles who do not know God;*

⁶ *that no one should take advantage of and defraud his brother in this matter, because the Lord is the avenger of all such, as we also forewarned you and testified.*

⁷ *For God did not call us to uncleanness, but in holiness.*

⁸ *Therefore he who rejects this does not reject man, but God, who has also given us His Holy Spirit.*

⁹ *But concerning brotherly love you have no need that I should write to you, for you yourselves are taught by God to love one another;*

¹⁰ *and indeed you do so toward all the brethren who are in all Macedonia. But we urge you, brethren, that you increase more and more;*

¹¹ *that you also aspire to lead a quiet life, to mind your own business, and to work with your own hands, as we commanded you,*

¹² *that you may walk properly toward those who are outside, and that you may lack nothing.*

8) What similarities do you see between this passage and Hebrews 13?

_____

_____

_____

Exploring the Meaning

9) Read 1 Timothy 6:6–11. How can the desire for worldly riches be a detriment to one's spiritual health and witness?

_____

_____

_____

10) Read Jude 24–25. How is this benediction like the one at the end of Hebrews? How is it different?

_____

_____

_____

Summing Up . . .

"We who are the true Christians have a serious responsibility to live spotlessly to the glory of God, so that unbelievers never have a just reason for criticizing the way we live, because how we live is a reflection on our Lord."—John MacArthur, *Hebrews*, Moody Press, 1983, p. 421.

Reflecting on the Text

11) If your life had been secretly videotaped for the last week, what activities or behaviors would you be ashamed of? What does this indicate in terms of any changes you need to make?

_____

_____

12) Who are two "brethren" who could use your love this week, and what are two practical ways you could demonstrate your care and compassion?

_____

_____

13) What are one or two of the most important lessons you have learned during your study of Hebrews?

_____

_____

14) What is one concrete way you want your life to be different in the future as a result of this study?

_____

_____

Recording Your Thoughts

For further study, see the following passages:

Leviticus 4:21; 16:27	Numbers 6:24–26	Psalm 118:6
Isaiah 63:11	Matthew 25:40, 45	John 13:35; 19:17
Acts 20:28	Romans 9:3–4; 12:3	Romans 14:17
1 Corinthians 8:8	2 Corinthians 13:14	Galatians 1:6–9
Ephesians 4:14	1 Timothy 3:2; 4:1–5	2 Timothy 2:4; 3:16
Titus 1:5–9	1 Peter 5:4	

The MacArthur Bible Collection

John MacArthur, General Editor

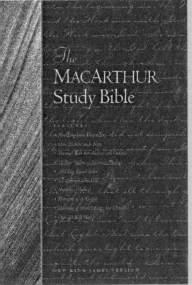

The MacArthur Study Bible

From the moment you pick it up, you'll know it's a classic. Featuring the word-for-word accuracy of the New King James Version, *The MacArthur Study Bible* is perfect for serious study. Pastor/teacher John MacArthur has compiled more than 20,000 study notes, a 200-page topical index and numerous charts, maps, outlines, and articles to create *The MacArthur Study Bible*. This Bible has been crafted with the finest materials in a variety of handsome bindings, including hardcover and indexed bonded leather. Winner of "The 1998 Study Bible of the Year Award."

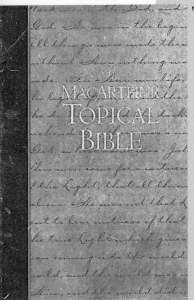

The MacArthur Topical Bible

In the excellent tradition of *Nave's Topical Bible,* this newly created reference book incorporates thousands of topics and ideas, both traditional and contemporary, for believers today and in the new millennium. Carefully researched and prepared by Dr. John MacArthur and the faculty of Masters Seminary, *The MacArthur Topical Bible* will quickly become the reference of choice of all serious Bible students. Using the New King James translation, this Bible is arranged alphabetically by topic and is completely cross-referenced. This exhaustive resource is an indispensible tool for the topical study of God's Word.

The MacArthur Bible Studies

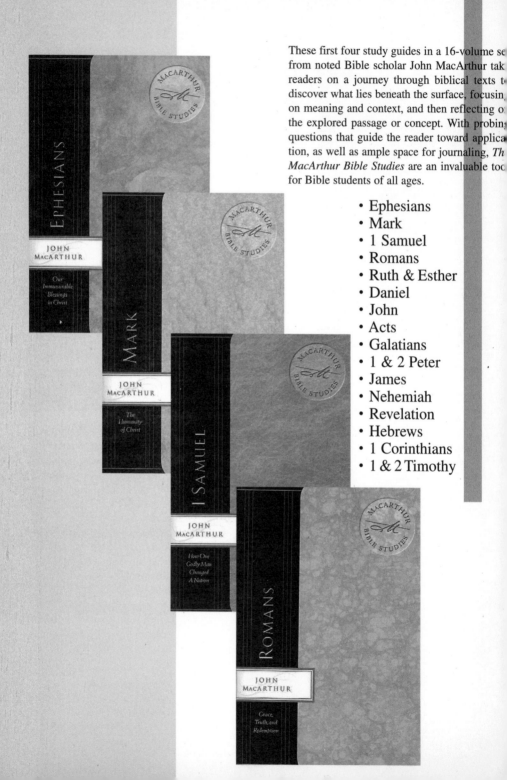

These first four study guides in a 16-volume se
from noted Bible scholar John MacArthur tak
readers on a journey through biblical texts t
discover what lies beneath the surface, focusin
on meaning and context, and then reflecting o
the explored passage or concept. With probin
questions that guide the reader toward applica
tion, as well as ample space for journaling, *Th*
MacArthur Bible Studies are an invaluable too
for Bible students of all ages.

- Ephesians
- Mark
- 1 Samuel
- Romans
- Ruth & Esther
- Daniel
- John
- Acts
- Galatians
- 1 & 2 Peter
- James
- Nehemiah
- Revelation
- Hebrews
- 1 Corinthians
- 1 & 2 Timothy